Emerald Home Lawyer

CONVEYANCING

A Practical Guide

Peter Wade

Emerald Publishing
www.emeraldpublishing.co.uk

Emerald Publishing
Brighton BN2 4EG

ISBN: 9781847161 03 1

Printed by GN Press Essex

Cover design by Emerald Graphics

Contents

1. Conveyancing of Registered Land   5

2. Acting for the Seller – Sellers Checklist   18

3. Exchanging Contracts   26

4. Acting for the Purchaser – Purchaser's Checklist   32

5. Acting for Seller in Freehold and Leasehold matters   35

6. Acting for Purchaser's   37

7. Council of Mortgage Lenders Handbook and   43
requirements

8. Completion and post completion   51

Glossary of terms
Standard conveyancing letters
Schedule of forms used in conveyancing

1

Conveyancing of Registered Land

Outline of a Conveyancing Transaction

A conveyancing transaction breaks down into three stages whether we are dealing with a sale or a purchase.

1. The pre-contract stage.

2. The time between exchange of contract and completion or pre-completion stage

   and

3. Post-completion stage.

The pre-contract stage is the longest and most complicated (contrary to what estate agents might tell you). Most of the legal work is done at this stage. Once contracts are exchanged things become time critical.

All of the delay takes place up to exchange of contracts and these can be attributable to things such as completing the chain of transactions, local authority searches time for everyone to obtain their mortgages. In a chain of transaction obviously the chain only proceeds at the pace of the slowest party.

OUTLINE OF A SALE

1. Taking instructions

2. Preparing pre-contract package to include office copy entries, fixtures and fittings list, sellers property information form

3. Exchange of Contracts

4. Approve transfer document

5. Answer Completion Information and Requisitions on Title

6. Prepare for completion

7. Completion

8. Post completion matters such as sending deeds to purchaser's solicitors pay off seller's mortgage.

OUTLINE OF PURCHASE

1. Take Instructions

2. Pre-contract searches and enquiries

3. Investigate title

4. Approve draft Contract

5. Exchange Contract

6. Prepare purchase deed

7. Pre completion searches

8. Prepare for completion

9. Complete

10. Post-completion matters such as pay Stamp Duty Land tax, register at land registry.

PRE-COMPLETION STAGE

The seller's solicitors must prepare a pre-completion package for the purchaser's solicitors

This consists of:

1. The draft contract which describes the land that is being sold and the price together with all the other terms of the transaction such as interest rates in the event of late completion, the amount of the deposit etc.

2. Evidence of the seller's title which nowadays usually consists of official office copies of the sellers' title at the land registry together with the filed plan.

3. Fixtures, fittings and contents list and solicitors property information form.

It may also include copy planning permissions, building regulations consents and guarantees.

Title

This usually consists of the official copies of the entries at the land registry but still may be unregistered title.

Searches

Any number of searches maybe obtained but the essential pre contract searches would be a local land charge search.

Other optional search's might be:

Water search

Environmental search

Mining search

Radon gas search

7

Finances

Most purchasers proceed with a mortgage provided by a bank or a building society.

Normally some sort of deposit is required, formerly ten-percent but now usually by negotiation.

The purchaser and his solicitor would need to be satisfied that sufficient funds are available to complete the purchase before contracts are exchanged.

Draft contract

This is the most important part of the transaction. Once the purchasers' solicitors are happy with the draft contract, it can then be prepared for exchange of contracts. The purchasers and sellers sign contracts in exactly the same format and they each sign their respective parts.

Once they are ready the solicitor will exchange the contract with a deposit changing hands.

Exchange of Contracts

This creates a binding contract. Neither party can then go back on the agreement without severe financial penalties.

Up until this point either party may withdraw from the transaction without any penalty.

The Home Information Pack aims to reduce the time between an offer for a property and exchange of contracts.

There are various methods of exchanging contracts which have been developed by solicitors. There are various formulae.

Much confusion surrounds the deposit. It is a part payment towards the purchase price and a form of security. The deposit will be forfeited if the purchaser withdraws. It is usually held by one of the solicitors as stakeholder which means it belongs to neither party until some other event happens such a completion.

Builders usually insist that their solicitors hold the deposit as agents' for the vendor. This has the risk that if the builder goes bust before completion that the purchaser may have lost his deposit, but once contracts are exchanged the purchaser may have a legitimate claim to the property.

From a legal and financial point of view exchange of contracts is the most important part of the transaction. As finances should have been set up completion is more of a practical part of the transaction that is the changing of funds and the moving in of the parties.

Post-Exchange of Contracts

Traditionally the purchasers' solicitor's raises requisitions on title. In the days of unregistered title this was a more onerous activity than nowadays. It should be an administrative matter to enquire as to the amount required at completion and where completion is to take place. It also deals with the undertaking to pay off mortgages.

Completion statement

If the property is leasehold then there will be a completion statement as items such as rent, service charge and insurance will need to be apportioned, that is worked out on a daily basis. The amount required by the seller's solicitors at completion should be checked carefully so as to obviate any problems that an incorrect figure may cause. It is good practice to confirm it in writing and to get the seller's solicitors to agree so as to avoid any shocks or misunderstandings.

The Purchase Deed

Now known as the TR1 for the transfer of the whole of a title which is the most common. This is a printed form which just has

9

to be competed with all the relevant information. A decision has to be made as to whether it should be signed by all the parties. If there is a covenant to observe previous restrictions then both sellers and purchasers need to sign.

It is the purchaser's duty to produce the purchase deed which is usually submitted in duplicate along with the requisitions on title. If approved the draft is used as the top copy. Care should be taken over spelling of names and the price as this is the document that will be submitted to the land registry and the opportunities to amend this document apart from minor amendments will be limited and could cause problems.

The seller must always sign the purchase deed as this is a basic requirement in the transfer of land.

MORTGAGE CONSIDERATIONS

The purchasers' solicitor is usually instructed by the lender to prepare the mortgage and obtain a good and marketable title for the lender. The lender secures his lending against the title by way of a legal mortgage. This is evidenced by the purchaser signing a mortgage deed and this being registered at the land registry as a charge.

The property cannot be sold without this charge being paid off. Lenders will normally only want and insist upon a first legal charge. This means they will have the right to enforce their charge by selling the property as mortgagee in possession in the event of the mortgage not being repaid.

In exchange for this the lender advances the money on the security of the property and the purchaser's solicitors' job is to make sure the funds are there at completion. The purchasers' solicitor will have to comply with all the conditions in the mortgage and submit a report on title. Once this has been accepted the funds will be available to complete

The purchasers' solicitors will have to undertake an extra search on behalf on the lender which is a bankruptcy search confirming the purchaser is not bankrupt.

PREPARING FOR COMPLETION

Prior to completion the final searches have to be undertaken which includes the bankruptcy search on behalf of the lender and a search of the title. This is a OS1 search which confirms that there have been no changes since the official copies were produced.

It has the second most important effect of giving the purchaser and his lender a priority period. This means during this period which will usually extend for at least thirty days no one else can register anything against this title.

During the period which should extend way beyond completion the purchaser should arranged for the stamp duty to be paid, the title to be registered at the land registry.

This is one of the most important aspects of searches, the priority periods and they should be noted in the diary carefully. Protection ends when the property period expires and you are taking a risk if you exceed the period as some other event can take place such as someone else registering a charge or any other kind of entry.

Discharge of sellers' Mortgage.

Most sellers have mortgages and this will need to be cleared on completion. The seller's solicitors will obtain the redemption figure that is the figure to clear the mortgage on completion.

Once this has been ascertained it is usually paid off on completion by telegraphic transfer. The seller's solicitors give an undertaking to do this and provide in due course either an END being a electronic notification of discharge or DS1 which is a paper discharge that needs to be lodged with the purchase document at the land registry

COMPLETION

These days this is a paperwork exercise technically the completion takes place at the sellers solicitors office where the balance of the purchase price is exchanged for the transfer deed, the discharge of the mortgage or an undertaking thereof any other title deeds and the keys.

The sellers solicitor undertakes that on receipt of the funds through the banking system that they will

1. Arrange for release of the keys which are usually held by the seller's estate agent.

2. Will date and forward the executed transfer deed.

3. Arrange to discharge the seller's mortgage

4. Give the purchasers solicitors an undertaking that the mortgage will be discharged.

5. Give a clear title to the purchaser that is discharge any other items on the title such as giving a clear receipt for any apportionments etc.

Clients think they have to attend completion but they need to be giving vacant possession of their existing property and taking possession of their new property. They will be informed by telephone of the transaction.

POST COMPLETION

Sellers Solicitors

1. Must redeem his client's mortgage.

2. Must obtain from the lender a receipt which he must send to the purchasers solicitors to show it has been redeemed either an end or DS1.

3. Pay any balance back to his client.

4. It is traditional that the seller's solicitor pays the estate agents commission account.

Buyers Solicitor

Prior to completion the purchasers solicitor must now obtain a form being an SDLT from meaning the stamp duty land tax form signed by the purchaser. This must be submitted to the Inland Revenue whether duty is payable or not.

The levels are up to £175,000 no duty thereafter 1% up to £250,00 then 3% up to £500,000 then 4% thereafter.

Application must be made to the land registry to register the transaction.

This will involve sending:

1. The fee

2. The transfer TR1

3. Evidence of any previous mortgage being paid off

4. Details of the new charge by delivery of a copy of the mortgage and the original mortgage.

The title can then be registered in the name of the new purchaser together with any charge.

Once registration is completed a copy should be sent to the purchaser for checking and any original documents should be sent to the lender for safekeeping.

Since the advent of dematerialization of title deeds these are less and less. The minimum that the lender will require is a copy of the new register entries. This will show that their charge has been correctly registered.

SALE AND PURCHASE.

Most transactions involve and sale and purchase.

Obviously the money from the purchase it tied up in the sale. All the above sale and purchase procedures need to be undertaken but all simultaneously that is why it is vital to have a foolproof method of exchanging contracts to make sure there are no hitches.

The National Conveyancing Protocol.

This was introduced in 1990 and was intended to standardise simplify and speed up domestic conveyancing transactions.

The protocol forms have already been mentioned such as fixtures fittings and contents form and seller's property information form. Also there is a standard form of contract.

In time it is assumed this will be totally replaced by the Home Information Pack.

LEGAL BACKGROUND TO CONVEYANCING

First Registration

1)   First registration must take place within two months of new triggers, first registration being amongst other things:

    a)   Deeds of Gift

    b)   Conveyances and Assignments

    c)   First Mortgagees

d)   Assents

e)   Vesting Assents

The Land Registry have issued a practice advice leaflet (No.14) which contains detailed guidance of these triggers.

The only estates capable of registration are legal fee simples and legal terms of years absolute.

That term exceeds 21 years.

Classes of Registered Title

- **Freehold absolute** – this is the best class of Title available. The Titleholder will take the legal estate, subject to any encumbrances protected by an entry on the register and overriding interest.

- **Freehold Possessory** – the registrar is not satisfied with the applicant's title, possessory title will be issued. The proprietor will take subject to any adverse interest, which exist or are capable of existing at the date of the first registration.

- **Freehold Qualified** – this title is very rare. It is for freehold land where there is defect or flaw affecting the applicant's title.

- **Leasehold Absolute** – This is terms or years equivalent to the freehold absolute class. If an unregistered lease with more than 7 years to run is assigned for value or by gift, it will be the subject to compulsory first registration.

- **Leasehold Possessory** – subject to any estate of interest that is adverse to the proprietor's title at the time of first registration.

- **Leasehold qualified** - the registrar believes that there is a flaw or defect in the leasehold title.

15

- **Good leasehold** – the registration is such that there is no guarantee that the lease has been invalidly granted, this will be issued when the registrar has not seen the superior title. The problem for this of course is that if the lease is held to be invalid, the lender will lose its security.

Preliminary matters – taking instructions

You should take as detailed instructions as possible at the outset. Constantly asking the client further questions undermines their confidence.

Tax and Planning Consequences

By obtaining full instructions other matters can be taken into account such as:

- Insuring the property

- Inheritance tax

- Co-ownership

- Planning

Take instructions in person where possible, in a personal interview.

Co-Sellers

Authority should be obtained from any co-seller or purchaser.

Status of the Conveyancer

The status of the conveyancer should be confirmed to the client and details of the complaints procedure given.

Protocol Forms

- The Seller's Property Information Form (4th Edition)

- Fixtures Fittings and Contents List (4th Edition)

- The Seller's Leasehold Information Form (3rd Edition)

These should be completed

Financial Charges

Details of all second and subsequent mortgages, improvement grants, discounts payable to the local authority and any other residents of the property should be established. Client care letters should be sent, giving estimate of charges etc.

Lender's requirements

Identity: the client must be verified in accordance with the Council of Mortgage Lenders Handbook. Taking any specific instructions to be included as special conditions.

Planning

The client should be asked the proposed use of the property, as it might require planning permission or affect restrictive covenants.

Tax

Does the transaction attract Capital Gains Tax, advise the client accordingly.

2

Acting For The Seller

It is now compulsory for all hones on the market in England and Wales that a Home Information Pack be provided.

WHAT ARE HIPS?

The Home information pack is compulsory for all homes on the market in England and Wales.

The documents provide the buyer with key information on the property and must be provided by the seller of the seller's agents.

You need a HIP because you cannot market your property without one.

The buyer's can see important information on the property at the start of the process, free of charge.

The idea behind this is that there is less chance of buyer's becoming aware of any surprise at the end of the process that can cause delay and extra expense to the buyer and the seller.

WHAT DOES THE HIP CONTAIN?

The Hip is set up between what is compulsory and what are the optional items.

The compulsory items in the HIP are for Freehold homes:
1. Home information pack

2. Energy performance certificate (EPC)
3. Sustainability information concerning new homes only
4. Sales statement
5. Evidence of Title – usually office copy entries
6. Standard searches – to include local authority, drainage and water

Leasehold Properties:

All the above plus a copy of the Lease.

There is optional documentation, which can be included in the HIP, these include:

Home condition report,
Legal summary,
Home/use contents form.

Other documents such as specialist reports.

Once the property is marketed the seller is responsible for commissioning the Hip by the time the property is on the market.

The seller pays for the HIP and the HIP is usually compiled by the estate agent, solicitor or a HIP provider.

BUYERS

If you are a buyer of a property you must be given a copy of the pack free of charge

WHEN SHOULD THE HIP BECOME AVAILABLE?

It must be available before the property is marketed for sale.

Article I.   SELLERS

Once the property is marketed the seller is responsible for commissioning the HIP by the time the property is on the market.

Article II.   WHO COMPILES THE HIP?

They can be done by an estate agent, solicitor or a HIP provider.

Article III.   WHO PAYS FOR THE HIP?

Payment for the HIP is the responsibility of the seller.

Sellers Checklist

- Client – full names and addresses of sellers, buyers home and business telephone numbers

- Estate agents details

- Where are the Title Deeds?

- Client's authority to obtain them

- Full address of the property

- Price

- Deposits

- Fixtures and Fittings

- Are they being removed?

- Any instructions on completion date

- Various use of the premises

- Who is resident at the premises

- Dependant on a purchase?

- Any other special conditions

- Any tenancy

- Advice as to Costs

- Any outstanding mortgages

- Where the proceeds of sale are to go

- Any C G T on sale proceeds

- Does it have to be synchronised with any other related purchase

- Obtain answers to Sellers Property Information Form and Fixtures, Fittings and Contents

- Check Identity of Client

SALES CONSIDERATIONS

- Request Title Deeds

- Request Office Copy Entries

- Draft Contract.

STANDARD CONDITIONS OF SALE (Fourth Edition)

Formerly contracts were headed Agreement, as we use terms like Exchange of Contracts, the word Agreement has been deleted.

Standard special conditions of the contract normally incorporate the Standard Conditions of Sale (Fourth Edition)

The Seller is to transfer the property with either full title guarantee or limited title guarantee, as specified on the front page of the Contract.

Standard conditions of sale set out all aspects of the transaction and the formation of the contract:

- Deposit

- Matters affecting the property

- Physical state

- Title and Transfer

Deposit

The buyer is to pay or send a deposit of 10% of the total of the purchase price and the Chattels price no later than the date of the contract.

Matters affecting the property

The property is sold free from encumbrances, other than those mentioned in the contract, those discoverable by inspection; those are available for inspection in the public register.

Physical State

The Buyer accepts the property in the physical state it is in at the date of the contract unless the seller is building or converting it.

Title and Transfer

The condition sets out how the seller will deduce title to both registered and unregistered land

Requisitions

The buyer may be precluded from raising requisitions on items that have been disclosed prior to exchange of contracts

Commonhold

This is under the Commonhold and Leasehold format 2002.The seller must provide a copy of the memorandum and articles of the common holders association and of the Commonhold community statement.

The front page of the contract sets out the sellers and buyers names.

The description of the property whether it is freehold or leasehold and its postal address.

Title number or Root of Title

Any specified Incumbrances

Title Guarantee – whether full or limited

When it has full title guarantee the seller has the right to dispose of the property and will at their own expense, make every reasonable effort to transfer the title offered, and the seller transfers free of all charges and encumbrances.

Limited title guarantee states that the transferor has not himself or herself encumbered the property and is not aware that anyone else has. An example of this would be a personal representative.

In leasehold titles both full and limited title guarantee imply that the lease is subsisting and that there is no existing breach that might result in forfeiture.

A plan is usually necessary for either transfer of whole or transfer of part, obviously more easily obtained now that most properties are registered. It is possible to obtain a plan from the Land

Registry by asking on the Index map search and this plan can be agreed for the transfer and the contract.

Sending the papers to the Purchaser Solicitors

- Draft contract in duplicate – you are recommended to keep your own file copy.

- The Protocol forms- Fixtures, Fittings and Contents, and Property Information Form

For Leasehold title, you would normally include

- Last service charge and three years accounts.

- Copy of Share Certificate of Management Company

- Copy of memorandum and articles of association

- Copy of block insurance policy and schedule

- Any guarantees, damp, timber, preservation etc

- Any copy of planning permission as building regulation consent

Further enquiries from purchaser's solicitors.

It is recommended that you take the client's express instructions concerning any replies to further enquiries.

The client will be liable for any misrepresentation in giving the reply.

If there has been any breach of planning or building regulation consent it is possible to obtain an indemnity.

Receiving Draft Contract

(Lack of proof from purchaser's solicitors?)

- Report to client on contract and obtain their execution thereof

- Confirm price, chattels, rates of interest etc with client.

If appropriate obtain client's instructions concerning a date for completion.

3

Exchange of Contracts

The Law Society's Formulae

Once the purchaser's and sellers are ready to exchange the buyer's solicitor indicates that the seller is now ready to commit to a binding contract.

Obviously once contracts have been exchanged, neither party will be able to withdraw from the contract, and therefore all documents and arrangements will need to be checked thoroughly.

If there is a dependant sale the solicitor must ensure that the exchange of contracts on both properties is synchronised to avoid leaving his client either owning two houses or being homeless.

If there is a failure of synchronisation it could be professional negligence.

Telephone

Exchange of contracts by telephone is the most common method of effecting an exchange.

Apart from a personal exchange no other method is entirely risk free. If contracts are exchanged at the telephone then the telephone conversation is the confirmation of exchange of contracts.

To avoid all uncertainties, the Law Society has agreed various formulae.

The most important aspect of using any of the formulae is an accurate attendance note recording the telephone conversation must be made as soon as practicable.

A typical memorandum of exchange would include:

- Date

- Time

- Wording of any variations

- Identity of any parties to the conversation.

- Purchase price - agree Deposit

Any variation of the formulae, such as reduced deposit, must be expressly agreed and noted in writing.

Law Society Formula A

This is for use when one solicitor holds both signed parts of the Contract.

The parties agree that exchange will take place from that moment and the solicitor holding both parts confirms that he or she undertakes by first class post or DX to send his or her signed part of the contract to the other solicitor, together with deposit as appropriate.

Law Society Formula B

For use where each solicitor holds his own client's signed part of the contract.

- Each solicitor confirms to the other that he or she holds the signed part of the agreed form signed by the clients, and will forthwith insert the agreed completion date.

- Each solicitor undertakes to send by first class post or DX his or her signed part of the contract to the other together with the deposit if appropriate.

Law Society Formula C

Part 1

Each solicitor confirms that he or she holds the part of the contract in agreed form signed by his or her client,

Each solicitor undertakes to the other that, they will hold that part of the contract until part 2 of the formula takes place.

Part 2

Each solicitor undertakes to hold part of the contract in his or her possession to the other's order, so that contracts are exchanged at that moment and to send it to the other on that day.

This is effectively the giving and receiving of a release, which is as important as exchanging contracts.

The parties have to comply with the release within the agreed time frame.

When synchronising you normally arrange to receive a release on your sales transaction from your buyer's solicitor, with say a time up to which it is effective.

When you have received your release on your sale you then give a release on your related purchase, with a slightly shorter time frame to allow you to exchange on the original transaction.

When your seller exchanges with you within the time that you have given to release you then go to your purchaser and exchange within the time on the release given to you.

It is obviously essential to make sure that once you have exchanged on your sale that you immediately exchange on purchase.

It is very important to have the terms of the release noted as carefully as if you were exchanging contracts, because one more phone call will then create an exchange of contract.

Client Care

Solicitors' Costs. Information and Client Care Code

The Client must be given cost information which must not be inaccurate or misleading, clearly in a way and a level which is appropriate to that particular client.

It should be confirmed in writing to the client as soon as possible. The basis of the firm's charges should be explained.

The solicitor should keep the client properly informed about costs as the matter progresses. The solicitor should tell the client, how much the costs are at regular intervals, like at least every six months and in appropriate cases delivering handbills at agreed intervals.

Complaints handling

The client must be told the name of the person in the firm to contact about any problems with the service provided.

The firm must have a written complaints procedure to ensure that the complaints are handled in accordance with it and ensure the client is given a copy of the complaints procedure on request.

Stamp Duty Land Tax

Stamp Duty Land Tax (SDLT) replaced Stamp Duty as from December 2003.

The rates of Tax are:

£0	-	£175,000	-	Nil	
£175,001	-	£250,000	-	1%	
£250,001	-	£500,000	-	3%	
£500,001	-	and above	-	4%	

This relates to a freehold transfer on the assignment on an existing lease.

Who should complete the Land Transaction Return?

It is the responsibility of the purchaser to make sure the information contained in the return is complete and correct, and is the purchaser who must sign the declaration on the return SDLT1.

Type of Property

Types of property are residential, mixed or non- residential

Description of transaction, every acquisition of a freehold or leasehold interest in land it also includes contract or agreement of the acquisition of such an interest where that contract is substantially performed.

Effective date of transaction.

The effective date will be the completion date or the earlier date of substantial performance.

About the Tax Calculation

There are designated disadvantaged areas and they will have a nil rate up to £150,000.

There is no need to forward the transfer or document of transfer, it is a tax on a transaction. There may not be in fact any document giving effect of the transaction.

It is a self-assessed tax and the burden of calculating any tax falls on the payer.

Whether or not any tax is payable a Land Transaction return in the appropriate form must be submitted to the revenue within 30 days of the chargeable event.

There are fines thereafter.

Sending in the return

Once the return is sent in and is correct a certificate will be issued.

This certificate will enable you to register the transaction with the Land Registry

4

Acting for the Purchaser-Purchasers Transaction Checklist

If you are a buyer of a property you must be given a copy of the Home Information Pack, free of charge. And the compulsory items in the Home Information pack for a freehold property are:

WHAT DOES THE HIP CONTAIN?

The Hip is set up between what is compulsory and what are the optional items.

The compulsory items in the HIP are for Freehold homes:

7. Home information pack
8. Energy performance certificate (EPC)
9. Sustainability information concerning new homes only
10. Sales statement
11. Evidence of Title – usually office copy entries
12. Standard searches – to include local authority, drainage and water

Leasehold Properties:

All the above plus a copy of the Lease.

There is optional documentation which can be included in the HIP, these include:

Home condition report,
Legal summary,
Home/use contents form.

Other documents such as specialist reports.

BUYERS CHECKLIST

- Existing client?

- Full names and address of the clients

- Estate agents details

- Freehold or Leasehold

- Price

- Any preliminary deposit paid

- Any fixtures and fittings being removed

- Any instructions on completion date

- Present or proposed use of the property

- Who is resident at the property

- How will any deposit be funded

- How is the balance of the purchase price to be funded – that is has the client obtained a mortgage

- Survey arrangements – is the property being surveyed?

- Give advice of types of survey

- How Is the property to be held – joint tenants or tenants in common

- Check clients identity in accordance with the CML handbook

5

Acting for the Seller in Freehold and Leasehold Matters

Sales transaction checklist – Sale of property-leasehold and freehold

- Seller

- Purchaser

- Purchasers solicitors

- Completion date.

1)   Take full instructions from client

2)   Obtain Title Deeds/Official copies of the Register

3)   Have Protocol Forms, property information and fixture, fittings and contents to be completed by client

4)   Send draft contract – Official copies of the Register – protocol forms to purchasers solicitors

5)   Obtain approval of draft contract from purchaser's solicitors

6)   Obtain and have contract signed by client

7)   Exchange contracts

8)   Request redemption figures for all charges on the property

35

9) Obtain estate agent's commission account

10) Reply to requisitions on title and approve draft transfer

11) Prepare bill and financial statement once the estate agents fee and redemption figure have been received

12) Obtain signature to the transfer

Completion

a) Forward a transfer and DS1/END to purchasers solicitors

b) Redeem existing mortgages either by cheque or CHAPS

c) Pay estate agent's account

d) Account for proceeds of sales to client

e) Receive DS1/END from mortgagee and forward to purchaser's solicitors in accordance with undertaking

6

Acting for the Purchasers of Freehold and Leasehold property

Purchase transaction checklist – Purchase of leasehold/freehold

- Purchaser

- Seller

- Completion date

- Take instructions

- Obtain funds for Local Authority search

- Water search

- Environmental search

- Receive the contract

- Protocol forms received

- Send local authority search

- Send environmental search

- Send water search

- Receive mortgage instructions

- Check conditions etc

- Report to client and obtain signature to contract

- Execution of mortgage

- Arrange completion date

- Exchange contracts

- Send report on title to lender

- Insure property

- Start any life policy necessary

- Raise requisitions and draft transfer

- Obtain execution of the transfer and forward to sellers solicitors

- Prepare bill and financial statements

- Send final searches OSI/ K16

- Receive any balance of purchase of monies required

- Receive mortgage advance

- Complete

- Pay Stamp Duty and forward SDLT form

- Once END/DS1 received, register at Land Registry

- Give notice of assignment of any lease if leasehold

- Completion of registration and forward Title Deeds to building society of if no mortgage to client

PURCHASERS IN FREEHOLD AND LEASEHOLD TRANSACTIONS

Receiving Draft paperwork

- Send copy plan to client

Checking

- Check main points of contract with client i.e. price, names to go in the contract

Searches

- Obtain fees from clients for searches being:

- Local search

- Environmental search

- Water search

- Coal mining search if necessary

- Commons registration search

When buying outside your area ask seller's solicitor's what are the usual searches?

- Local land charge search – this will reveal

  a) Planning permissions

  b) Buildings regulation consent

  c) If road adopted

  d) Any road proposals

  e) Any enforcement or planning notices

- Environmental search

- Coal search will reveal whether it is a coal mining area

Raising any preliminary enquiries

Official copy entries to the Title

- You should check

   a) Description of the land according to the contract description

   b) Title number

   c) Estate – freehold or leasehold

   d) Easements

   e) Any rights of way

   f) Flying freeholds

Proprietorship register

- Is the class of Title correct

- Is the seller the registered proprietor

- Any cautions or other entries on the Title

- Undertaking or release of the caution will be required

- Note any restrictive covenants referred to on the Title and advise the client, as this may affect their use and enjoyment of the premises. There may be covenants not to erect anything on the premises without the original owners consent

- Any missing covenants then consider an indemnity

- Any recent sales of the property as an under-value or no value.

- Consider insolvency of seller

Contract/ Agreement

- Check the name of the seller is the same as the proprietorship register

- Similarly Title number

- Check special conditions

Protocol Forms

- Fixtures fitting and contents – this is usually an extra to the contract to incorporate the chattels.

- Obtain client's approval of this prior to exchange of contracts

- Sellers Property Information Form (SPIF) check

    a) Boundaries

    b) Any guarantees

    c) Occupiers

    d) Any changes to the property for planning purposes

    e) Any disputes

Leasehold sellers

- Leasehold information form

- Leasehold enquiries - assignment of lease. The information required by the purchaser's solicitors is similar to a freehold transaction, with the additional details of the lease to be bought.

Items to be checked

- Landlord's consent required

- Length of the residue of term to be checked

- The lender may have specific requirements

- Check plan accurately identifies the property

- Any restrictions on sub-letting i.e. last 7 years

- Does the description of the property conform with the plan

- Does the assignee have to enter into a direct covenant with the landlord. Are there covenants to enforce on behalf of the landlord

- Any covenants against the other tenants

- Check insurance complies with the lenders requirements

- Check service charge accounts for the last three years including receipt for the last sum payable.

- Request whether there is any potential change in the next year.

- Obtain receipt from last rent – similarly service charge

- Check whether any apportionment required

- Check whether any alterations to the premises, which would require landlords, consent.

7

Council Of Mortgage Lenders Handbook(CML Handbook)

The lender's handbook provides comprehensive instructions for conveyancers acting on behalf of lenders in residential conveyancing transactions.

It is divided into two parts

Part 1 sets out the main instructions

Part 2 details each lenders specific requirements relating to the main instructions. (last updated 13th October 2003).

There is a chance of a conflict of interest because you are acting for both the borrower and the lender. If there is any conflict of interest you should refuse to act for one or other of the parties.

You can only reveal information to the lender if the borrower agrees, if the borrower refuses to agree you must return mortgage instructions to the lender.

Communications

All communications with the lender must be in writing, quoting the mortgage account or roll number and the clients name etc.

Safeguards

* A proof of identity of borrowers

* You must follow the guidance of the Law Society's green card (mortgage fraud) and pink card (undertakings under Money Laundering Regulations 1993)

- Proof of identity can be one from List A and two from List B

- List A – valid full passport – valid HM Forces identity card – valid UK Photocard – Driving Licence – any other document in additional list A part two.

- List B – cheques guarantee card- Mastercard or Visa, American Express, Diners Card. All firearms or shotgun certificates or

  a) Receipted utility bill less than three months old

  b) Or council tax bill less than three months old

  c) Rent book

  d) Mortgage statement

Valuation of the property.

The borrower should be advised not to rely upon the report

Re-inspection

Where a final inspection is needed you must ask for the final inspection at least 10 working days before the advance is required.

Title and surrounding circumstances

If the owner or registered proprietor has been registered for less than six months, or if the seller is not the registered proprietor this must be reported unless - the person represented is the registered proprietor of an institution or mortgagee exercising power of sales are receiving bankruptcy, liquidator or developer or builder, selling the property under part exchange scheme.

Searches and reports

You must make all the usual necessary searches and enquiries.

A lender should be named as the applicant in the HM Land Registry search.

All searches except where there is a priority, period must be no more than six months old at completion

All of the searches such as mining searches should be undertaken in the areas affected and for personal searches and search insurance, they should be checked in part two.

Planning and Building Regulations

* The property must have the benefit of any necessary planning consent

* Having a good and marketable title

* The title of the property must be good and marketable, free of any restrictions, covenants, easement, charges or encumbrances, which might reasonably be expected to adversely affect the value of the property.

Flying Freeholds

Freehold flats and other freehold arrangements. Each individual lender will have its own requirements.

Restrictions on use and occupation

Any material restrictions on its use should be reported, such as occupier's employment, age or income.

Restrictive Covenants

You must enquire whether the property is being built, altered or is currently used in breach in of a restrictive covenant.

First Legal Charge

They require a fully enforceable first charge by way of legal mortgage over the property. All existing charges must be redeemed on or before completion.

Leasehold Property

A period of an unexpired lease as set out in part two. There must be no provision for forfeiture on insolvency of the tenant or any superior tenant. There must be satisfactory legal rights for access services, support, shelter and protection.

There must be adequate covenants in respect of building insurance, maintenance, repair of structure, foundations, main walls, roof etc.

You should ensure that responsibility of the insurance, maintenance and repair of the services is through the common services that of the landlord or one or more of the tenants of the building that forms one or more of a management company.

The lease must contain adequate provisions for the enforcement of these obligations of the landlord or Management Company.

If the terms of the lease are unsatisfactory, you must obtain a suitable deed of variation, or indemnity insurance: see part two.

You must obtain on completion the clear receipt or written confirmation of the last payment of ground rent and service charge from the landlord or the managing agent.

Notice of the mortgage must be served on the landlord or any management company.

It must be reported if the landlord is either absent or insolvent

A recent article in the Law Society Gazette stated that a frequent ground for complaint arises when insufficient checks are made by buyer's solicitors to ensure that ground rent, service charges and other outgoings relating to leasehold purchases are paid up to date on completion.

It is both prudent and good practice for the buyer's solicitors to contact the managing agents for the properties directly or to ensure that the seller's solicitors do so.

Solicitors will then be able to ensure that the documentary evidence is available in relation to the payment of ground rents and service charges including apportionment's where appropriate. They can also confirm whether the freehold holder or superior landlord is planning any future improvement or remedial work and can consider the benefit if negotiating a retention with landlord's solicitors to protect their client's. A solicitors omission to seek and to clarify information available from managing agents may result in inadequate professional service.

Management company

The Management Company must have the legal right to enter the property.

You should make a company search and prove that the company is in existence and registered at Company's House.

You should obtain the management companies last three years published accounts.

INSOLVENCY CONSIDERATIONS

You must obtain a clear Bankruptcy search against the borrower.

You must certify that any entries do not relate to the borrower.

If the property is subject to deed of gift or transaction at an apparent undervalue, completed in under five years of the proposed mortgage you must be satisfied that the lender will be protected, if not arrange indemnity insurance.

You must obtain a clear bankruptcy search against all parties between a deed of gift or transaction that is an apparent under value.

POWERS OF ATTORNEY

Any document that is being executed under a Power of Attorney, you must ensure that the Power of Attorney is properly drawn, appears to be properly executed and the Attorney knows of no reason why such Power of Attorney will not be subsisting at completion.

Power of Attorney must not be used in connection with a regulated loan under the Consumer Credit Act 1974.

The original certified copy of the Power of Attorney must be sent with the deeds.

THE PROPERTY

Boundaries

These must be clearly defined by reference to a suitable plan or description.

Purchase price

This must be the same as set out in the instructions. Must advise the lender if there are any cash back or non-cash incentives.

Vacant possession

It is the term of the loan that Vacant possession is obtained unless otherwise stated.

New Properties

You must ensure that there is a National House Building Council Buildmark Scheme or similar.

Roads and Sewers

If not adopted, there must be a suitable agreement or a bond in existence.

Easements

All reasonable steps to check the property has the benefit of all easements.

Insurance

Where the lender does not arrange any insurance this must be arranged so that cover starts no later than completion.

Other occupiers

Rights of interested persons who are not a party to the mortgage who are or who will be in occupation of the premises may affect their right and you must obtain a signed deed or form of consent from all occupants age 17 or over.

Signing and Witnessing of Documents

Witnessing of documents is considered good practice so that the signature of a document that needs to be witnessed is witnessed by a solicitor, legal executive or licensed conveyancer.

All documents required at completion must be dated with the date of completion of the loan.

After completion you must register the mortgage with the HM Land Registry.

Your mortgage file.

For evidential purposes you must keep your file for at least six years from the date of the mortgage before destroying it.

Legal Costs

All charges and disbursements are payable by the buyer and should be collected on or before completion.

Non payment of fees or disbursements should not delay the stamping and registration of documents.

8

Completion and Post-Completion

Between exchange of contracts and completion –Preparing for Completion-Sellers checklist

- Check Transfer has been approved and requisitions replied to

- Received engrossed transfer from buyer – sign plan of the transfer.

- Seller to execute transfer in time for completion.

- Obtain mortgage redemption figure from mortgagees relating to all mortgages

- For leasehold obtain last receipts and make any apportionment necessary

- Prepare completion statement where necessary and send copies to buyer's solicitor in time for completion.

- Prepare an undertaking that needs to be given on completion for discharge of mortgage

- Locate title deeds and schedule to be handed over on completion

- Check arrangements for vacant possession and handing over keys

- Ensure estate agents are aware of completion arrangements

- Prepare bill and send to client

DOCUMENTS TO BE HANDED OVER ON COMPLETION

- Title deeds if unregistered, no land or charge certificate since October 2003, due to de-materialisation of deeds.

- END/ DS1 or undertaking

- Any money received for fixtures and fittings

- Arrange for keys to be released by agents

BETWEEN EXCHANGE OF CONTRACTS AND COMPLETION – PREPARING FOR COMPLETION – BUYERS CHECKLIST

- Transfer approved and requisitioned satisfactorily answered

- Give power to execute mortgage deed

- Purchase deed and plan

- Send executed transfer to sellers solicitors in sufficient time for his client to sign prior to completion

- Do pre-completion searches – such as bankruptcy, OS1 for purchaser whole, OS2, purchaser part.

- Company search

- Make report on title to lender and request advance cheque in time for completion

- Received completion statement where necessary

- Remind client of arrangements for completion

- Check property insured

- Check arrangements for vacant possession and handing over of keys

- Ensure estate agents are aware on completion arrangements

- Make arrangements for transmission of completion money to sellers solicitors on the day of completion or where he has directed

AFTER COMPLETION – SELLERS CHECKLIST

- Confirm receipt of funds

- Telephone buyer's solicitors

- Telephone estate agent to confirm completion and authorise release of keys

- Inform client that completion has taken place

- Send Title Deeds and other relevant documents by first class post. DX on date of completion

- Transfer any purchase funds on related purchase

- Discharge existing mortgage by CHAPS or cheque with END or DS1 as required

- Pay estate agent's commission account

- Account to client for balance of proceeds of sale

- Transfer costs if agreed

- On receipt of DS1 or confirmation of END send or inform purchaser's solicitors and ask to be released from undertaking previously given to them.

- Remind client to cancel buildings insurance and notify public utilities

- Remind client of any Capital Gains Tax assessment which may be due

- Check file before placing in dead system

AFTER COMPLETION – BUYERS CHECKLIST

- Inform Client and Lender that completion has taken place

- Complete Mortgage Deed

- Complete file copies of Mortgage Deed and other relevant documents

- Arrange payment of Stamp Duty on the SDLT form. As this form now has to be signed by the purchaser's it would be wise to have this signed prior to completion at the same time as the transfer.

- If acting for a Company, register charge at Company's House within 21 days. This time limit is absolute and cannot be extended without an order of the court. Failing to register within the time limit will be an act of negligence by the solicitor.

- Pay off and deal with any undertakings concerning finance. Once SDLT form clear by the Revenue, and you are in receipt of the DS1 or END, register at Land Registry.

- On receipt of DS1 or confirmation of END, release seller's solicitors from their undertaking.

- Make application for Registration of Title within the relevant priority period.

- Serve a notice of assignment of Life policies or lease.

- On receipt of Title Information document from the Land Registry, check contents carefully.

- Deal with the custody of Deeds in accordance with the client's instructions or send to Lender to be held by them during the continuance of the Mortgage.

Glossary

A

Acting for both parties

There are limited circumstances when solicitors can act for both parties

Amount outstanding on the mortgage

Also known as the redemption figure

Apportionment of the purchase price

This may be used to save stamp duty land tax Fixtures and fittings known as chattels do not attract stamp duty and this is why the distinction between those and land is important.

Attorneys

A deed may be signed by an attorney but evidence of his power of attorney must be produced as this will be required by the land registry.

Auctions

The auction contract is usually prepared in advance The purchaser has the right to undertake all his searches en enquiries and survey before the auction. Once the auction has been concluded usually a ten per cent deposit is taken and the sale takes place 28 days later. It would be necessary for anyone entering into an auction to have their finance in place before the hammer falls.

B

Boundaries

Even with a registered title the boundaries shown on the filed plan are general boundaries and are not definitive. The rule is generally what has been there for the last 12 years is the boundary this may have to be supported by statutory declarations.

Breach of a Restrictive Covenant

Or other defect. Indemnity insurance might be available

Bridging Finance

This might be for a deposit which is repaid on the sale of the property. It is rare for English banks to extend finance for a property that is open ended. It is usually only extended once contracts are exchange and there is a fixed date for completion.

Building Regulation Consent

This may be required even if there are not developments that require planning permission. It relates to health and safety matters and the type of materials used on completion of building works for which consent it required a final certificate must be obtained from the local authority. This is evidence that the building regulations have been complied with.

C

Capital Gains Tax

The main exemption which affects residential conveyancing is the principal private dwelling house exemption The seller must have occupied the dwelling house as his only or main residence throughout the period of ownership There is a sliding scale for absences and exemptions of short periods of absence

Capacity

The seller might be sole owner, joint owner, personal representative mortgagee, charity, company bankrupt or otherwise incapacitated.

Classes of Title

There are different classes of title the best being absolute title but there is also possessory title qualified title and good leasehold title

Contaminated Land

Any contamination could have serious effects in that it may be impossible to sell or obtain a mortgage on.

Completion

The day on which the transaction is finalised, the money changes hands and the parties vacate and take possession of the land that is the moving day.

Co-Ownership

This is where more than one person owns the land such as tenant in common or joint tenant.

Conveyancing

The process of transferring the ownership of freehold and leasehold land.

Compulsory Registration

This has arisen since 1990 and applies to the whole of England and Wales. The categories of events triggering a registration have changed but it is still not compulsory to register land without one of these triggers but voluntary registration could take place.

Conservation Area

Any non listed building in a conservation area must not be demolished with conservation area consent. There are also restrictions on development.

Contract Races

This is where more than one contract has been issued solicitors are obliged to let both parties know the terms of the race that is what needs to be done to secure the property. It must be confirmed in writing. A standard contact race would specific that the first person to be in a position to exchange contracts unconditionally wins the race. This is usually signified by the purchasers solicitors producing a signed contract and deposit cheque together with authority to proceed.

Covenants

This is a promise made in a deed and binding any subsequent owner of the land they may include such matter as maintaining the fences and only using the land for the erection of one property.

D

Deeds

Apart from unregistered land most deeds have now dematerialised as they are registered at the land registry. Evidence of ownership is shown by official copies of the registered entries. This is an official dated document showing the current state of the title.

Deposit

Although not a legal requirement is it customary and it's a form of security and part payment towards the purchase price.

Discharge of seller's mortgage

On completion is the seller has a mortgage this will need to be paid off and evidence given to the purchasers solicitor. This will need to be lodged at the land registry as proof of the discharge before a new purchaser can be substituted and maybe a new mortgage started.

Draft contract

The name attached to the contract before it is agreed by the parties and prior to exchange of contracts. Once the contract is approved it can be signed by the parties and forms the basis of the transactions. They must be in the same format. Identical contracts are exchanged.

E

Easements

This is a right over land of another such as a right of way or of light.

Engrossment

Merely means s properly types up version of a document the draft is amended then the engrossment is the fair copy

Escrow

A document such as contract mortgage transfer is delivered and will not become effective until some future date. It is therefore held in escrow the condition being that the event takes place such as completion or exchange of contracts. Gets rid of the need for all the parties to a transaction being in the same room at the same time.

Exchange of contracts

When the parties agree to bind themselves legally to buy and sell the land.

Execution

Means the signing of a document in a certain way for a deed to be valid it must contain the words this deed signed by the necessary parties in the presence of a witness and be delivered.

F

Filed plan

In conveyancing a plan is a map showing the land referred to edged in red. It is the official designation of the land for land registry purposes

Fixture and fittings

Now a formal part of the process in that purchasers solicitor will expect to see a completed fixtures and fittings form. It may be acceptable to apportion part of the price for fixtures and fittings and this is sometimes undertaken when the price falls on one of the bands for change in stamp duty. The list must be legitimate ad the revenue have the right to query this and levy any tax not paid

Fixtures and fittings distinction

Between objects not attached to the land are fittings and those attached are fixtures. The current fixtures and fitting list covers most eventualities but care should be taken if an offer is deemed to include items at the property they should be specifically mentioned in the contract.

Full Survey

As the name suggests this is full survey of the property and should contain a detailed breakdown of every aspect of the property.

H

Home Buyers Valuation and Survey Report

This is a compromise between a full structural survey and valuation.

I

Insurance

The risk on the property passes when contracts are exchanged. Even thought he purchaser has not got possession. The property is usually also insured by the seller up until the date of completion. They both have an insurable risk.

Indemnity Covenants

Any owner of land will remain liable for the covenants and passes these on by way of an indemnity covenant by any incoming purchaser

Investigating Title

Once the seller has produced the contract package the purchasers solicitors investigate title. This is to ensure that the seller is the owner of the property which is the subject of the contract. Also it must not reveal any defects other than those can be rectified prior to exchange of contracts.

There may for instance be consent required from a third party such as the necessity to register the transfer of a lease and become the member of a management company.

J

Joint tenants

This is most common between husband and wife. Both own equal shares in the property if either were to die the other inherit by way of survivorship. They cannot leave their share by will to anyone else.

L

Listed Building

Where a building might be of outstanding historic or architectural important the secretary of state may list it. Any alterations to the property will require both planning permission and listed building consent.

M

Mortgage

Is where the owner of land borrows money on the security of the land Also known as a legal charge. The lender has certain statutory powers the most important being that they can sell the property in the event of the loan not being paid.

Mortgage Fraud

Normally some proof of identity is required but this has been overtaken by the money laundering rules whereby it is accepted practice that clients should produce to their solicitors all the usual forms of ID to include utility bills driving licence passport etc.

Mortgages Repayments

The main types of repayment are pension, endowment and interest only. They do not affect the conveyancing transaction but some may have slightly different procedures between the conveyancers and the lender such as notices or deposit of insurance policies.

O

Occupiers Rights

The most important is the spouse of the seller. They have a statutory right to occupy the matrimonial home. Usually an enquiry is made as to there being any other occupiers of the matrimonial home. They are then asked to sign the contract to confirm they will give vacant possession completion.

Office Copy Entries

Usually refers to the registered title but can relate to any official copy issued by the land or other registries. They are acceptable as the originals.

Overriding Interests

These are matters affecting the land which are not on the register although this is being resolved under the current land registry rules. The most important being rights of way not mentioned on the deeds local land charges squatters rights.

P

Planning - Use of the property

It should be checked that the property has permission for its current use. Any purchaser should be aware that any change of use form its current use may require planning permission. For example a residential property may not be used for the fixing and selling of cars without a change of use. Any breach will be enforced by the local planning authority.

Planning Breach

This could be rectified by retrospective permission or again by indemnity insurance.

Purchase Deed

Now the transfer or TR1 this is the document that is signed by the seller transferring the land from the seller to the purchaser. It is signed prior to completion and once the formalities have been finalised such as the passing of the money it will be forwarded to the purchasers solicitors. This document will need to be stamped and registered at the land registry.

Possessory Title

The registry may grant a possessory title in the event of lack of paper title and eventually it can be upgraded to an absolute title. Land can be acquired through adverse possession but it is still subject to all covenants and easements etc existing at the date of the registration

Post Contact Stage

Between exchange of contracts and completion essential things such as finance is resolved as our final searches and all documents signed in readiness for completion.

R

Radon

If the property is in an area affected by radon gas a specific search should be undertaken which will reveal whether a survey has been undertaken and remedial measures have been taken.

Registered land

A state run system that proves the ownership of land by have a title registered at the HM land registry.

S

Searches

There are a series of searches. Before exchange of contracts the local authority search, after exchange bankruptcy and land registry searches.

Special Conditions

Any special condition will be used to vary the standard conditions of sale contained in the contract

Subject to Contract

This is of historical interest now as it is not possible to exchange contracts inadvertently or entering into irrevocably buying land without a proper contract. Some organisations still insist on using it as it gives them comfort Not now necessary in view of the Law Of Property (Miscellaneous) Provisions act 1989

Survey

There are many kinds of survey form the mere valuation by a lender to a full structural survey. Any purchaser should be aware that at the moment the law says *caveat emptor* that is let the buyer beware. Apart form a deliberate misstatement the seller is not liable for the current state of the property. An invariable practice is for purchasers to be advised to have a survey of the property and not to rely solely on the building society valuation.

Title

Either the registered or unregistered proof of the seller's ownership of the land.

Title Number

Every piece of registered land has a unique title number and must be used in all official documents searches etc.

Tenants in Common

Is where two or more people own land jointly in separate shares. Either owner can pass their share by will to anyone they wish.

Tenure

The legal term for how the land is being held being either freehold or leasehold.

U

Unregistered Land

The seller has to prove title by a series of documents such as conveyances, mortgagees etc now being replaced by registered conveyancing.

Undertakings

These are promises by solicitor to undertake certain acts. The most common being that the sellers solicitor will discharge the existing mortgage. Failure to comply with the undertaking is a professional offence so therefore they will not be entered into lightly and can be relied up They should always be confirmed in writing and their terms made certain.

Upgrading Title

Either on application or on the initiative of the registrar a title may be upgraded such as possessory to absolute and the same for qualified and good leasehold title

V

Valuation

Can either be an estate agents valuation which is a financial matter for the purchasers and sellers a lenders valuation is the figure that is used to calculate how much the lender is prepared to lend. This is based on a valuers report prepared for the lender once the buyer has requested a loan. It is an assessment of the value not a survey of the property. Lenders will normally exclude liability for any defects in the property. They are not undertaking that the property is fit for its purpose just because they are prepared to lend on it.

Value Added Tax – VAT

Is payable on solicitors costs but not o the purchase price of second hand properties. There is not VAT payable on stamp duty or land registry fees in a domestic transaction.

W

Witnesses

Must be a responsible adult and is usually independent of the parties who must add name, address and occupation

SALE 0F PROPERTY

STANDARD LETTERS

Letter to Building Society / Bank Requesting Title Deeds

22 February, 2009

Address

Dear Sirs

Re   Property:
**   Account Number:**
**   Borrower:**

We act for the above named clients in connection with the sale of the above property and we shall be obliged if you would please send us have the Title Deeds relating to this property.

We undertake to hold them to your order pending redemption of the mortgage.

At the same time please let us know the amount owing under this mortgage.

Yours faithfully

Letter to Estate Agent Acknowledging Sales Particulars

22 February, 2009

Address

Dear Sirs

Re **Property:**
Our Client:

We acknowledge safe receipt of your sales particulars and we confirm we have today contacted the purchaser's solicitors with a view to issuing a draft Contract.

Yours faithfully

Authority to Bank to Obtain Title Deeds

22 February, 2009

Address

Dear Sirs

We hereby give you authority to release the Title Deeds for property listed below to .... of ....

Address of Property: ....

Address of Lender: ....

Account Number: ....

Signature   ....

Signature   ....

First Letter to Purchaser's Solicitors

22 February, 2009

Address

Dear Sirs

Re   Property:
Your Client:
Our Client:

We understand that you act on behalf of ??????? of ?????????????? in connection with their proposed purchase of the above from our clients ??????????????.

We would be obliged if you could confirm that if your clients have a property to sell a purchaser has been found and if your client should require finance this has been approved at least in principle.

Subject to the above being confirmed we will arrange for a draft Contract to be issued to you as soon as possible.

Yours faithfully

Letter Issuing Contract etc to Purchaser's Solicitors

22 February, 2009

Address

Dear Sirs

Re   Property:
Your Client:
Our Client:

Thank you for your letter of ????????. We take this opportunity of enclosing:

1. Draft Contract in duplicate

2. Official Copy of Register Entries plus File Plan

3. Fixtures Fittings and Contents List

4. Seller's Property Information Form

5. Copy Transfer dated ???????????

Yours faithfully

Letter to Purchaser' Solicitor on Completion

22 February, 2009

Fax & Post

Fax Number: ....

Address

Dear Sirs

Re   Property:
     Your Client:
     Our Client:

We acknowledge safe receipt of your Telegraphic Transfer in the sum of £........ and we take this opportunity of enclosing the following:

1. TR1

2. Land Certificate number ....

3. All Pre-registration documents

Kindly acknowledge safe receipt.

We confirm that we have today telephoned the agents to release the keys.

Yours faithfully

Letter Sending Approved TR1 and Replies to Requisitions on Title

22 February, 2009

Address

Dear Sirs

Re   Property:
         Your Client:
         Our Client:

Thank you for your letter of .... we take this opportunity of enclosing the following:

1. TR1 approved as amended

2. Requisitions on Title and our replies thereto

Yours faithfully

Letter to Purchaser's Solicitor on Exchange of Contracts

22 February, 2009
Fax & Post
Fax Number:

Address

Dear Sirs

Re   **Property:**
         Your Client:
         Our Client:

Further to our telephone conversation at 2:15 p.m. between ......
and .... Contracts were exchanged and the date fixed
for completion is ....

The sale price is £........ and you will be holding the £.........
deposit strictly to our order pending completion.

We enclose our client's part of the Contract to complete
exchange of Contracts. .

Yours faithfully

Letter to Estate Agents requesting Commission Account

22 February, 2009

Address

Dear Sirs

Re   Property:
Client:

We write to confirm Contracts have now been exchanged in this matter. The date fixed for completion being the ....

We await hearing from you with your commission account.

Yours faithfully

Letter to Bank/Building Society Requesting Redemption Figure

22 February, 2009

Building Society
Address

Dear Sirs

Re: Borrower:
Property:
Account No:

Would you please let us have the redemption figure on the above mortgage account as at *date*.......

Yours faithfully

Letter Informing Utilities of Sale

22 February, 2009

Address

Dear Sirs

Re   Owner:
Property:
Account No:

We take this opportunity of advising you that the above property has now been sold and as from .... the new occupants will be ....

Yours faithfully

Letter to Seller's Solicitor on Exchange of Contracts

22 February, 2009
Fax & Post
Fax Number:

Address

Dear Sirs

Re   Property:
**   Your Client:**
**   Our Client:**

Further to our telephone conversation at 2:15 p.m. between ......
and .... Contracts were exchanged and the date fixed
for completion is ....

The purchase price is £....... and we will be holding the £........
deposit strictly to your order pending completion.

We enclose our client's part of the Contract to complete
exchange of Contracts. .

Yours faithfully

Letter to Seller's Solicitors Sending TR1 with Requisitions on Title

22 February, 2009

Address

Dear Sirs

Re   Property:
        Your Client:
        Our Client:

Thank you for your letter of .... we take this opportunity of enclosing the following:

1. TR1 in duplicate

2. Requisitions on Title

Yours faithfully

Letter to Seller's Solicitor Confirming Purchase Money Sent

22 February, 2009
Fax & Post
Fax Number:

Address

Dear Sirs

Re   Property:
**   Your Client:**
**   Our Client:**

We are writing to confirm we have today telegraphically transferred to you the sum of £……….. being the balance required to complete this matter.

We await hearing from you with a dated and executed Transfer and all the other Title Deeds relating to the property.

We would be obliged if on receipt of the money you could kindly telephone the agents to release the keys.

Yours faithfully

SCHEDULE OF DOCUMENTS TO BE USED IN CONVEYANCING

1) PROTOCOL FORMS

   a) Fixtures, Fittings and Contents (4th Edition)

   b) Sellers Property Information Form (4th Edition)

   c) Sellers Leasehold Information Form (3rd Edition)

2) General Leasehold Enquiries

3) Land Registry Forms

   a) TR1

   b) TP1

   c) OS1

   d) OS2

   e) SIM

   f) FR1

   g) OC1

   h) DS1

   i) AP1

   j) D1

4) Various Search Forms

   a) Local Authority Search LLC1

   b) Standard Enquiries for Local Authority (2002 edition)

5)   Stamp Duty Land Tax – Land transaction return (SDLT1) and Self Certificate SDLT60

6)   Completion Information and Requisitions on Title

7)   Draft contract

Assents, 15

Bankruptcy search, 48
Boundaries, 41, 48, 57
Buildings regulation consent, 39
Buyers Solicitor, 13

Capital Gains Tax, 17, 54, 57
Coal search, 40
Commonhold, 23
Complaints handling, 29
Completion, 3, 6, 9, 35, 36, 37, 38, 51, 58, 74, 86
Consumer Credit Act 1974, 48
Co-ownership, 16
Co-Sellers, 16

Deeds of Gift, 14
Discharge of sellers' Mortgage, 11
Draft contract, 8, 24, 60, 86

Easements, 40, 49, 60
Energy performance certificate, 19, 32
Environmental search, 7, 37, 39, 40
Escrow, 60
Exchange Contract, 6
Exchange of Contracts, 6, 8, 9, 21, 26, 76, 82

Financial Charges, 17
First Legal Charge, 46
First Registration, 14
Fixtures Fittings and Contents List, 17, 73
Flying freeholds, 40
Freehold absolute, 15
Freehold Possessory, 15
Freehold Qualified, 15

Good leasehold, 16

Home information pack, 18, 19, 32

Inheritance tax, 16
Insurance, 49, 62
Insuring the property, 16

Law Society's Formulae, 26
Leasehold Absolute, 15
Leasehold Possessory, 16
Leasehold qualified, 16
Legal Costs, 50
Lender's requirements, 17

Management company, 47
Mining search, 7
Money Laundering Regulations 1993, 43

Planning, 16, 17, 39, 45, 64
Post-completion stage, 5
Power of Attorney, 48
Pre completion searches, 6
Proprietorship register, 40
Protocol Forms, 17, 35, 41
Purchase price, 27, 49

Radon gas search, 7
Requisitions, 6, 23, 75, 83, 86
Requisitions on Title, 6, 75, 83, 86
Restrictive Covenants, 45

Searches, 7, 39, 45, 66
Sellers Solicitors, 13
Stamp Duty Land tax, 6
Standard Conditions of Sale, 22

Status of the Conveyancer, 17

Taking instructions, 5
Tax and Planning Consequences, 16
The draft contract, 7
The National Conveyancing Protocol, 14
The pre-contract stage, 5
The Purchase Deed, 10
The Seller's Leasehold Information Form, 17
The Seller's Property Information Form, 17
Title, 7, 15, 19, 20, 21, 22, 23, 32, 35, 38, 40, 41, 44, 52, 53, 54, 55, 58, 62,
    65, 66, 67, 69, 71, 84
Title Guarantee – whether full or limited, 23

Vacant possession, 49
Valuation of the property, 44

Water search, 7, 37, 39

Land Registry
Application for an official search of the index map

If you need more room than is provided for in a panel, and your software allows, you can expand any panel in the form. Alternatively use continuation sheet CS and attach it to this form.

Land Registry is unable to give legal advice but our website www1.landregistry.gov.uk provides guidance on Land Registry applications. This includes public guides and practice guides (aimed at conveyancers) that can also be obtained from any Land Registry office.

See www1.landregistry.gov.uk/regional if you are unsure which Land Registry office to send this application to.

Where there is more than one local authority serving an area, enter the one to which council tax or business rates are normally paid.

If no postal address insert description, for example 'land adjoining 2 Acacia Avenue'.

1	Local authority serving the property:

2 Property to be searched

Flat/unit number:

Postal number or description:

Name of road:

Name of locality:

Town:

Postcode:

Ordnance Survey map reference (if known):

Known title number:

3 Application and fee

See fees calculator at www1.landregistry.gov.uk/fees

Application	Fee paid (£)
Search of the index map	

Fee payment method

Place 'X' in the appropriate box.

The fee will be charged to the account specified in panel 4.

☐ cheque made payable to 'Land Registry'

☐ Land Registry credit account

☐ direct debit, under an agreement with Land Registry

Peapod Solutions Ltd.

	4	This application is sent to Land Registry by

4 This application is sent to Land Registry by

If you are paying by direct debit, this will be the account charged.

Key number (if applicable):

Name:

Address or UK DX box number:

Email address:

Reference:

Phone no: Fax no:

Please note that the facility of issuing results electronically is not available at present. When it is, a direction will appear on our website and details will be given in Public Guide 1 and Practice Guide 10. Until there is a direction, you do not need to complete this panel to obtain an official copy in paper format.

Official copies issued electronically are in 'Portable Document Format' (PDF) which replicates the appearance of the hard copy version. You will need Adobe Acrobat Reader (which you can install free from www.adobe.com) to open the document.

Place 'X' in the box if applicable.

5 Issue of certificate of result of search in paper format where an email address has been supplied

If you have supplied an email address in panel 4, then, unless you complete the box below, any certificate of result of search of the index map will be issued electronically to that address, if there is a direction under section 100(4) of the Land Registration Act 2002 by the registrar covering such issuing.

☐ I have supplied an email address but require the certificate of result of search to be issued in paper format instead of being issued electronically

Any attached plan must contain sufficient details of the surrounding roads and other features to enable the land to be identified satisfactorily on the Ordnance Survey map. A plan may be unnecessary if the land can be identified by postal description.

6 I apply for an official search of the index map in respect of the land referred to in panel 2 shown   on the attached plan

7

Signature of applicant: --

Date:

WARNING

If you dishonestly enter information or make a statement that you know is, or might be, untrue or misleading, and intend by doing so to make a gain for yourself or another person, or to cause loss or the risk of loss to another person, you may commit the offence of fraud under section 1 of the Fraud Act 2006, the maximum penalty for which is 10 years' imprisonment or an unlimited fine, or both.

Failure to complete this form with proper care may result in a loss of protection under the Land Registration Act 2002 if, as a result, a mistake is made in the register.

Under section 66 of the Land Registration Act 2002 most documents (including this form) kept by the registrar relating to an application to the registrar or referred to in the register are open to public inspection and copying. If you believe a document contains prejudicial information, you may apply for that part of the document to be made exempt using Form EX1, under rule 136 of the Land Registration Rules 2003.

Land Registry
Application for first registration

FR1

You must lodge the documents of title with this application; these must be listed on Form DL.

If you need more room than is provided for in a panel, and your software allows, you can expand any panel in the form. Alternatively use continuation sheet CS and attach it to this form.

Land Registry is unable to give legal advice but our website www1.landregistry.gov.uk provides guidance on Land Registry applications. This includes public guides and practice guides (aimed at conveyancers) that can also be obtained from any Land Registry office.

See www1.landregistry.gov.uk/regional if you are unsure which Land Registry office to send this application to.

'Conveyancer' is a term used in this form. It is defined in rule 217(1) of the Land Registration Rules 2003 and includes, among others, solicitor, licensed conveyancer and fellow of the Institute of Legal Executives.

LAND REGISTRY USE ONLY
Record of fees paid
Particulars of under/over payments
Reference number
Fees debited £

Where there is more than one local authority serving an area, enter the one to which council tax or business rates are normally paid.

1 Local authority serving the property:

Insert address including postcode (if any) or other description of the property, for example 'land adjoining 2 Acacia Avenue'.

On registering a rentcharge, profit a prendre in gross or franchise, insert a description, for example 'Rentcharge (or as appropriate) over 2 Acacia Avenue'.

2 Property:

Place 'X' in the appropriate box. Only use the third option where the property has an address and is fenced on the ground.

Enter reference, for example 'edged red'.

Enter nature and date of document.

3 The extent of the land to be registered can be clearly identified on the current edition of the Ordnance Survey map from

☐ the attached plan and shown:

☐ the plan attached to the:

☐ the address shown in panel 2

Place 'X' in the appropriate box.

4 The class of title applied for is ☐ absolute leasehold
☐ absolute freehold ☐ good leasehold
☐ possessory freehold ☐ possessory leasehold

5 Application, priority and fees

Applications in priority order	Price paid/Value (£)	Fees paid (£)
First registration of the freehold/leasehold estate		
	Total fees (£)	

See fees calculator at www1.landregistry.gov.uk/fees

Fee payment method

☐ cheque made payable to 'Land Registry'

Place 'X' in the appropriate box.

The fee will be charged to the account specified in panel 7.

☐ direct debit, under an agreement with Land Registry

Peapod Solutions Ltd.

Provide the full name(s) of the person(s) applying to change the register. Where a conveyancer lodges the application, this must be the name(s) of the client(s), not the conveyancer.

Complete as appropriate where the applicant is a company. Also, for an overseas company, unless an arrangement with Land Registry exists, lodge either a certificate in Form 7 in Schedule 3 to the Land Registration Rules 2003 or a certified copy of the constitution in English or Welsh, or other evidence permitted by rule 183 of the Land Registration Rules 2003.

6	The applicant:

For UK incorporated companies/LLPs
Registered number of company or limited liability partnership including any prefix:

For overseas companies
(a) Territory of incorporation:

(b) Registered number in England and Wales including any prefix:

If you are paying by direct debit, this will be the account charged.

This is the address to which we will normally send requisitions and return documents. However if you insert an email address, we will use this whenever possible..

7	This application is sent to Land Registry by

Key number (if applicable):

Name:

Address or UK DX box number:

Email address:
Reference:

Phone no:	Fax no:

Place 'X' in the appropriate box.

In this and panel 10, each proprietor may give up to three addresses for service, one of which must be a postal address whether or not in the UK (including the postcode, if any). The others can be any combination of a postal address, a UK DX box number or an electronic address.

8	The address(es) for service for each proprietor of the estate to be entered in the register is

☐ the address of the property (where this is a single postal address)

☐ the following address(es):

Where the applicant is more than one person, place 'X' in the appropriate box.

Complete as necessary.

9	Where the applicant is more than one person

☐ they hold the property on trust for themselves as joint tenants

☐ they hold the property on trust for themselves as tenants in common in equal shares

☐ they hold the property on trust:

Where a charge has an MD reference we will ignore an address given in this panel unless the charge is in favour of a United Kingdom bank and neither the charge form nor any agreement we have with the lender specifies an address for service.

For permitted addresses see note to panel 8.

Complete as appropriate where the proprietor of the charge is a company. Also, for an overseas company, unless an arrangement with Land Registry exists, lodge either a certificate in Form 7 in Schedule 3 to the Land Registration Rules 2003 or a certified copy of the constitution in English or Welsh, or other evidence permitted by rule 183 of the Land Registration Rules 2003.

10	Name and address(es) for service for the proprietor of any charge to be entered in the register:

For UK incorporated companies/LLPs
Registered number of company or limited liability partnership including any prefix:

For overseas companies
(a) Territory of incorporation:

(b) Registered number in England and Wales including any prefix:

If this statement applies (i) place 'X' in the box and (ii) enclose Form DI.

Rule 28 of the Land Registration Rules 2003 sets out the disclosable overriding interests that you must tell us about.

11 Disclosable overriding interests

☐ Disclosable overriding interests affect the estate.

12 Certificate

The title is based on the title documents listed in Form DL which are all those under the control of the applicant.

Details of rights, interests and claims affecting the estate (other than non-disclosable interests falling within rule 28(2) of the Land Registration Rules 2003) known to the applicant are, where applicable, disclosed in the title documents and Form DI if accompanying this application.

☐ The applicant knows of no other such rights, interests and claims. Only the applicant is in actual possession of the property or in receipt of the rent and profits from the property.

☐ The applicant knows only of the following additional such rights, interests and claims, including those of any person (other than the applicant) in actual possession of the property or in receipt of the rent and profits from the property:

13 Examination of title

☐ I/we have not fully examined the applicant's title to the estate, including any appurtenant rights, or satisfied myself/ourselves that it has been fully examined by a conveyancer in the usual way prior to this application.

14 Confirmation of identity

When registering transfers, charges, leases and other dispositions of land, Land Registry relies on the steps that conveyancers take, where appropriate, to verify the identity of their clients. These checks reduce the risk of property fraud.

Full details of the evidence of identity that is required can be found in Practice Guide 67 and in Public Guide 20.

Where a person was not represented by a conveyancer, Land Registry requires 'evidence of identity' in respect of that person, except where the first alternative in panel 13(2) applies.

'Evidence of identity' is evidence provided in accordance with any current direction made by the Chief Land Registrar under section 100(4) of the Land Registration Act 2002 for the purpose of confirming a person's identity.

The requirement of registration is contained in section 4, Land Registration Act 2002. Further guidance is contained in Practice Guide 1.

If this application is to register a transfer, lease or charge, dated on or after 10 November 2008 **and** the requirement of registration applies, complete one of the following

Place 'X' in the appropriate box.

☐ I am a conveyancer, and I have completed panel 15

Conveyancer is defined in rule 217(1) of the Land Registration Rules 2003 and includes, among others, solicitor, licensed conveyancer and fellow of the Institute of Legal Executives.

☐ I am not a conveyancer, and I have completed panel 16

15 Where the application is sent to Land Registry by a conveyancer

(1) Details of conveyancer acting

If you are sending an application to register a transfer, lease or charge, for each party to each disposition that is to be registered state in the table below the details of the conveyancer (if any) who represented them.

Where a party is not represented by a conveyancer you must also complete (2) below.

Place 'X' in the box in the second column if the person or firm who is sending the application to Land Registry represented that party in the transaction. Otherwise complete the details in the third column. If the party is not represented insert 'none' in the third column.

Name of transferor, landlord, transferee, tenant, borrower or lender		Conveyancer's name, address and reference
	☐	Reference:
	☐	Reference:
	☐	Reference:

(2) Evidence of identity

Where any transferor, landlord, transferee, tenant, borrower or lender listed in (1) was not represented by a conveyancer

Place 'X' in the appropriate box(es).

☐ I confirm that I am satisfied that sufficient steps have been taken to verify the identity of

Insert the name of each unrepresented transferor, landlord, transferee, tenant, borrower or lender for whom you give this confirmation.

----

and that they are the transferor, landlord, transferee, tenant, borrower or lender listed in (1) (as appropriate)

Evidence of identity is defined in panel 14. Full details of the evidence of identity that is required can be found in Practice Guide 67.

☐ I enclose evidence of identity in respect of each unrepresented transferor, landlord, transferee, tenant, borrower or lender for whom I have not provided the confirmation above

16 Where the application is sent to Land Registry by someone who is not a conveyancer

(1) Details of conveyancer acting

If you are sending an application to register a transfer, lease or charge (ie a mortgage), for each party to each disposition that is to be registered, state in the table below the details of the conveyancer (if any) who represented them.

You must also complete (2) below.

If the party is not represented insert 'none' in the second column.

Name of transferor, landlord, transferee, tenant, borrower or lender	Conveyancer's name, address and reference
	Reference:
	Reference:
	Reference:

(2) Evidence of identity

Place 'X' in the appropriate box(es).

☐ for each applicant named in panel 6 is enclosed

Evidence of identity is defined in panel 14. Full details of the evidence of identity that is required can be found in Practice Guide 20.

☐ for each unrepresented transferor, landlord, transferee, tenant, borrower or lender listed in (1) is enclosed

If a conveyancer is acting for the applicant, that conveyancer must sign.	17

Signature of conveyancer: ----------------------------------

Date:

OR

If no conveyancer is acting, the applicant (and if the applicant is more than one person then each of them) must sign.

Signature of applicant: ----------------------------------

Date:

WARNING

If you dishonestly enter information or make a statement that you know is, or might be, untrue or misleading, and intend by doing so to make a gain for yourself or another person, or to cause loss or the risk of loss to another person, you may commit the offence of fraud under section 1 of the Fraud Act 2006, the maximum penalty for which is 10 years' imprisonment or an unlimited fine, or both.

Failure to complete this form with proper care may result in a loss of protection under the Land Registration Act 2002 if, as a result, a mistake is made in the register.

Under section 66 of the Land Registration Act 2002 most documents (including this form) kept by the registrar relating to an application to the registrar or referred to in the register are open to public inspection and copying. If you believe a document contains prejudicial information, you may apply for that part of the document to be made exempt using Form EX1, under rule 136 of the Land Registration Rules 2003.

CON 29R Enquiries of local authority (2007)

The Law Society

A duplicate plan is required for all searches submitted directly to a local authority.
If submitted manually, this form must be submitted in duplicate. Please type or use BLOCK LETTERS

A.

Local authority name and address

Search No:

Signed:

On Behalf of:
Local authority/private search company/member of the
public (indicate as appropriate)

Dated:

B.

Address of the land/property

UPRN(s):
Secondary name/number:
Primary name/number:
Street:
Locality/village:
Town:
Postcode:

C.

Other roadways, footways and footpaths in
respect of which a reply to Enquiry 2 is required

D.

Fees
£_____
is enclosed/paid by NLIS transfer (delete as applicable)

Signed:

Dated:

Reference:

Tel. No:

Fax No:

E-mail:

E. (For HIPs regulations compliance only)

Names of those involved in the sale (this box is only
completed when the replies to these enquiries are to be
included in a Home Information Pack)

Name of vendor:

Name of estate agents:

Name of HIP provider:

Name of solicitor/conveyancer:

Your personal data - name and address - will be handled strictly in accordance
with the requirements of the Data Protection Act. It is required to pass on to the
relevant authority(ies) in order to carry out the necessary searches

F.

Reply to

DX address:

Notes

A. Enter name and address of appropriate Council. If the
property is near a local authority boundary, consider raising
certain enquiries (e.g. road schemes) with the adjoining
Council.
B. Enter address and description of the property. Please
give the UPRN(s) (Unique Property Reference Number)
where known. A duplicate plan is required for all searches
submitted directly to a local authority. The search may be
returned if land/property cannot easily be identified.
C. Enter name and/or mark on a plan any other roadways,
footways and footpaths abutting the property (in addition to
those entered in Box B) to which a reply to enquiry 2 is
required.
D. Details of fees can be obtained from the Council, your
chosen NLIS channel or search provider.
E. BOX E is only to be completed when the replies to these
enquiries are to be included in a Home Information Pack. Enter
the name of the individual(s) and firms involved in the sale of
the property.
F. Enter the name and address/DX address of the person or
company lodging or conducting this enquiry.

CON 29R Enquiries of the Local Authority (2007)

PLANNING AND BUILDING REGULATIONS

1.1. Planning and building decisions and pending applications

Which of the following relating to the property have been granted, issued or refused or (where applicable) are the subject of pending applications

(a) a planning permission
(b) a listed building consent
(c) a conservation area consent
(d) a certificate of lawfulness of existing use or development
(e) a certificate of lawfulness of proposed use or development
(f) building regulations approval
(g) a building regulation completion certificate
(h) any building regulations certificate or notice issued in respect of work carried out under a competent person self-certification scheme

1.2. Planning designations and proposals

What designations of land use for the property or the area, and what specific proposals for the property, are contained in any existing or proposed development plan?

Roadways, footways and footpaths

Which of the roads, footways and footpaths named in the application for this search (via boxes B and C) are:

(a) highways maintainable at public expense
(b) subject to adoption and, supported by a bond or bond waiver
(c) to be made up by a local authority who will reclaim the cost from the frontagers
(d) to be adopted by a local authority without reclaiming the cost from the frontagers

OTHER MATTERS

3.1. Land required for public purposes

Is the property included in land required for public purposes?

3.2. Land to be acquired for road works

Is the property included in land to be acquired for road works?

3.3. Drainage agreements and consents

Do either of the following exist in relation to the property

(a) an agreement to drain buildings in combination into an existing sewer by means of a private sewer
(b) an agreement or consent for (i) a building, or (ii) extension to a building on the property, to be built over, or in the vicinity of a drain, sewer or disposal main

3.4. Nearby road schemes

Is the property (or will it be) within 200 metres of any of the following

(a) the centre line of a new trunk road or special road specified in any order, draft order or scheme
(b) the centre line of a proposed alteration or improvement to an existing road involving construction of a subway, underpass, flyover, footbridge, elevated road or dual carriageway;
(c) the outer limits of construction works for a proposed alteration or improvement to an existing road, involving (i) construction of a roundabout (other than a mini roundabout) or (ii) widening by construction of one or more additional traffic lanes
(d) the outer limits of (i) construction of a new road to be built by a local authority (ii) an approved alteration or improvement to an existing road involving construction of a subway, underpass, flyover, footbridge, elevated road or dual carriageway (iii) construction of a roundabout (other than a mini roundabout) or widening by construction of one or more additional traffic lanes
(e) the centre line of the proposed route of a new road under proposals published for public consultation
(f) the outer limits of (i) construction of a proposed alteration or improvement to an existing road involving construction of a subway, underpass, flyover, footbridge, elevated road or dual carriageway (ii) construction of a roundabout (other than a mini roundabout) (iii) widening by construction of one or more additional traffic lanes, under proposals published for public consultation

3.5. Nearby railway schemes

Is the property (or will it be) within 200 metres of the centre line of a proposed railway, tramway, light railway or monorail?

3.6. Traffic Schemes

Has a local authority approved but not yet implemented any of the following for the roads, footways and footpaths (named in Box B) which abut the boundaries of the property

(a) permanent stopping up or diversion
(b) waiting or loading restrictions
(c) one way driving
(d) prohibition of driving
(e) pedestrianisation
(f) vehicle width or weight restriction
(g) traffic calming works including road humps
(h) residents parking controls
(i) minor road widening or improvement
(j) pedestrian crossings
(k) cycle tracks
(l) bridge building

3.7. Outstanding notices

Do any statutory notices which relate to the following matters subsist in relation to the property other than those revealed in a response to any other enquiry in this form

(a) building works
(b) environment
(c) health and safety
(d) housing
(e) highways
(f) public health

3.8. Contravention of building regulations

Has a local authority authorised in relation to the property any proceedings for the contravention of any provision contained in Building Regulations?

3.9. Notices, orders, directions and proceedings under Planning Acts

Do any of the following subsist in relation to the property, or has a local authority decided to issue, serve, make or commence any of the following

(a) an enforcement notice
(b) a stop notice
(c) a listed building enforcement notice
(d) a breach of condition notice
(e) a planning contravention notice
(f) another notice relating to breach of planning control
(g) a listed building repairs notice
(h) in the case of a listed building deliberately allowed to fall into disrepair, a compulsory purchase order with a direction for minimum compensation
(i) a building preservation notice
(j) a direction restricting permitted development
(k) an order revoking or modifying planning permission
(l) an order requiring discontinuance of use or alteration or removal of building or works
(m) a tree preservation order
(n) proceedings to enforce a planning agreement or planning contribution

3.10. Conservation area

Do the following apply in relation to the property

(a) the making of the area a conservation area before 31 August 1974
(b) an unimplemented resolution to designate the area a conservation Area

3.11. Compulsory purchase

Has any enforceable order or decision been made to compulsorily purchase or acquire the property?

3.12. Contaminated land

Do any of the following apply (including any relating to land adjacent to or adjoining the property which has been identified as contaminated land because it is in such a condition that harm or pollution of controlled waters might be caused on the property)

(a) a contaminated land notic
(b) in relation to a register maintained under section 78R of the Environmental Protection Act 1990
    (I) a decision to make an entry
    (ii) an entry
(c) consultation with the owner or occupier of the property conducted under section 78G(3) of the Environmental Protection Act 1990 before the service of a remediation notice

3.13. Radon gas

Do records indicate that the property is in a 'Radon Affected Area' as identified by the Health Protection Agency?

CON 29O Optional enquiries of local authority (2007)

The Law Society

A duplicate plan is required for all searches submitted directly to a local authority.
If submitted manually, this form must be submitted in duplicate. Please type of use BLOCK LETTERS.

A.

Local authority name and address:

B.

Address of the land/property

UPRN(s):

Secondary name/number:

Primary name/number:

Street:

Locality/village:

Town:

Postcode:

C.

Optional Enquiries
(please tick as required)

☐   4.   Road proposals by private bodies
☐   5.   Public paths or byways
☐   6.   Advertisements
☐   7.   Completion notices
☐   8.   Park and countryside
☐   9.   Pipelines
☐   10.   Houses in multiple occupation
☐   11.   Noise abatement
☐   12.   Urban development areas
☐   13.   Enterprise zones

D.

Fees £
is enclosed/paid by NLIS transfer (delete as applicable)

Signed:

Dated:

Reference:

Phone No:

Fax No:

E-mail:

☐   14.   Inner urban improvement areas
☐   15.   Simplified planning zones
☐   16.   Land maintenance
☐   17.   Mineral consultation areas
☐   18.   Hazardous substance consents
☐   19.   Environmental and pollution notices
☐   20.   Food safety notices
☐   21.   Hedgerow notices
☐   22.   Common land, town and village greens

E.

Reply to:

DX address:

NOTES:
A. Enter name and address of appropriate Council. If the property is near a local authority boundary, consider raising certain enquiries (e.g. road schemes) with the adjoining Council.
B. Enter address and description of the property. Please quote the UPRN(s) (Unique Property Reference Number) where known. **A duplicate plan is required for all searches submitted directly to a local authority.** The search may be returned if land/property cannot easily be identified.
C. Enquiries 1-3 appear on CON29R Enquiries of local authority.
D. Details of fees can be obtained from the Council, your chosen NLIS channel or search provider.
E. Enter the name and address /DX address of the person or company lodging or conducting this enquiry.

CON29O Optional enquiries of local authority (2007)

ROAD PROPOSALS BY PRIVATE BODIES

4. What proposals by others, still capable of being implemented, have the Council approved for any of the following, the limits of construction of which are within 200 metres of the property

(a) The construction of a new road

(b) The alteration or improvement of an existing road, involving the construction, whether or not within existing highway limits, of a subway, underpass, flyover, footbridge, elevated road, dual carriageway, the construction of a roundabout (other than a mini roundabout) or the widening of an existing road by the construction of one or more additional traffic lanes

This enquiry refers to proposals by bodies or companies (such as private developers) other than the Council (and where appropriate the County Council) or the Secretary of State.

A mini roundabout is a roundabout having a one-way circulatory carriageway around a flush or slightly raised circular marking less than 4 metres in diameter and with or without flared approaches.

PUBLIC PATHS OR BYWAYS

5.1. Is any footpath, bridleway, restricted byway or byway open to all traffic which abuts on, or crosses the property, shown in a definitive map or revised definitive map prepared under Part IV of the National Parks and Access to the Countryside Act 1949 or Part III of the Wildlife and Countryside Act 1981?

5.2. If so, please mark its approximate route on the attached plan

ADVERTISEMENTS

Entries in the register

6.1. Please list any entries in the register of applications, directions and decisions relating to consent for the display of advertisements.

6.2. If there are any entries, where can that register be inspected?

Notices, proceedings and orders

6.3. Except as shown in the official certificate of search:

(a) has any notice been given by the Secretary of State or served in respect of a direction or proposed direction restricting deemed consent for any class of advertisement

(b) have the Council resolved to serve a notice requiring the display of any advertisement to be discontinued

(c) If a discontinuance notice has been served, has it been complied with to the satisfaction of the Council

(d) have the Council resolved to serve any other notice or proceedings relating to a contravention of the control of advertisements

(e) have the Council resolved to make an order for the special control of advertisements for the area

COMPLETION NOTICES

7. Which of the planning permissions in force have the Council resolved to terminate by means of a completion notice under s.94 of the Town and Country Planning Act 1990?

PARKS AND COUNTRYSIDE

Areas of outstanding natural beauty

8.1. Has any order under s.82 of the Countryside and Rights of Way Act 2000 been made?

National Parks

8.2. Is the property within a National Park designated under s.7 of the National Parks and Access to the Countryside Act 1949?

PIPELINES

9. Has a map been deposited under s.35 of the Pipelines Act 1962, or Schedule 7 of the Gas Act 1986, showing a pipeline laid through, or within 100 feet (30.48 metres) of the property?

HOUSES IN MULTIPLE OCCUPATION

10. Is the property a house in multiple occupation, or is it designated or proposed to be designated for selective licensing of residential accommodation in accordance with the Housing Act 2004?

NOISE ABATEMENT

Noise abatement zone

11.1. Have the Council made, or resolved to make, any noise abatement zone order under s.63 of the Control of Pollution Act 1974 for the area?

Entries in register

11.2. Has any entry been recorded in the noise level register kept pursuant to s.64 of the Control of Pollution Act 1974?

11.3. If there is any entry, how can copies be obtained and where can that register be inspected?

URBAN DEVELOPMENT AREAS

12.1. Is the area an urban development area designated under Part XVI of the Local Government, Planning and Land Act 1980?

12.2. If so, please state the name of the urban development corporation and the address of its principal office.

ENTERPRISE ZONES

13. Is the area an enterprise zone designated under Part XVIII of the Local Government, Planning and Land Act 1980?

INNER URBAN IMPROVEMENT AREAS

14. Have the Council resolved to define the area as an improvement area under s.4 of the Inner Urban Areas Act 1978?

SIMPLIFIED PLANNING ZONES

15.1. Is the area a simplified planning zone adopted or approved pursuant to s.83 of the Town and Country Planning Act 1990?

15.2. Have the Council approved any proposal for designating the area as a simplified planning zone?

LAND MAINTENANCE NOTICES

16. Have the Council authorised the service of a maintenance notice under s.215 of the Town and Country Planning Act 1990?

MINERAL CONSULTATION AREAS

17. Is the area a mineral consultation area notified by the county planning authority under Schedule 1 para 7 of the Town and Country Planning Act 1990?

HAZARDOUS SUBSTANCE CONSENTS

18.1. Please list any entries in the Register kept pursuant to s.28 of the Planning (Hazardous Substances) Act 1990.

18.2. If there are any entries:

(a) how can copies of the entries be obtained

(b) where can the register be inspected

ENVIRONMENTAL AND POLLUTION NOTICES

19. What outstanding statutory or informal notices have been issued by the Council under the Environmental Protection Act 1990 or the Control of Pollution Act 1974?

(This enquiry does not cover notices under Part IIA or Part III of the EPA, to which enquiries 3.12 or 3.7 apply.)

FOOD SAFETY NOTICES

20. What outstanding statutory notices or informal notices have been issued by the Council under the Food Safety Act 1990 or the Food Hygiene Regulations 2006?

HEDGEROW NOTICES

21.1. Please list any entries in the record maintained under regulation 10 of the Hedgerows Regulations 1997.

21.2. If there are any entries:

(a) how can copies of the matters entered be obtained

(b) where can the record be inspected

COMMON LAND AND TOWN OR VILLAGE GREEN

22.1. Is the property, or any land which abuts the property, registered common land or town or village green under the Commons Registration Act 1965 or the Commons Act 2006?

22.2. If there are any entries, how can copies of the matters registered be obtained and where can the register be inspected?

---

(1) References to the provisions of particular Acts of Parliament or Regulations include any provisions which they have replaced and also include existing or future amendments or re-enactments.

(2) The replies will be given in the belief that they are in accordance with information presently available to the officers of the replying Council but none of the Councils or their officers accept legal responsibility for an incorrect reply, except for negligence. Any liability will extend to the person who raised the enquiries and the person on whose behalf they were raised. It will also extend to any other person who has knowledge (personally or through an agent) of the replies before the time when he purchases, takes a tenancy of, or lends money on the security of the property (if earlier) the time when he becomes contractually bound to do so.

(3) This Form should be read in conjunction with the guidance notes available separately.

(4) 'Area' means any area in which the property is located.

(5) References to 'the Council' include any predecessor Council and also any council committee, sub-committee or other body or person exercising powers delegated by the Council and their "approval" includes their decision to proceed. The replies given to certain enquiries cover knowledge and actions of both the District Council and County Council.

(6) Where relevant, the source department for copy documents should be provided.

Fittings and contents form

Document date [ ][ ] / [ ][ ] / [ ][ ]

Address of the property

Postcode [ ][ ][ ][ ][ ][ ][ ][ ]

This form should be completed and read in conjunction with the explanatory notes available separately

1 Central heating and hot water

	Included	Excluded	None	Comments
Immersion heater	☐	☐	☐	
Hot water tank/cylinder	☐	☐	☐	
Hot water tank/cylinder jacket	☐	☐	☐	
Wall heaters	☐	☐	☐	
Night storage heaters	☐	☐	☐	
Gas fires (with any surround)	☐	☐	☐	
Electric fires (with any surround)	☐	☐	☐	
Roof insulation	☐	☐	☐	
Free-standing heaters	☐	☐	☐	

2 Electrical

	Included	Excluded	None	Comments
Electric points	☐	☐	☐	
Electric switches	☐	☐	☐	
Dimmer switches	☐	☐	☐	

The Law Society

www.hips.lawsociety.org.uk

TA10

© Law Society 2007
Peapod Solutions Ltd

3 Interior light fittings

	Included	Excluded	None	Comments
Ceiling lights	☐	☐	☐	
Wall lights	☐	☐	☐	
Lamp shades	☐	☐	☐	

Note: If light fittings are to be removed, it is assumed that they will be replaced by ceiling rose and socket, flex, bulb holder and bulb.

4 Television and telephone

	Included	Excluded	None	Comments
Television aerial	☐	☐	☐	
Radio aerial	☐	☐	☐	
Telephone receivers	☐	☐	☐	
Satellite dish	☐	☐	☐	

5 Windows

	Included	Excluded	None	Comments
Double glazing	☐	☐	☐	
Windows and window fitments	☐	☐	☐	
Shutters/grills	☐	☐	☐	

6 Doors

	Included	Excluded	None	Comments
Internal doors	☐	☐	☐	
External doors	☐	☐	☐	
Door knockers	☐	☐	☐	
Doorbell/chimes	☐	☐	☐	

	Included	Excluded	None	Comments
Garden shed	☐	☐	☐	
Greenhouse	☐	☐	☐	
Garden furniture	☐	☐	☐	
Garden ornaments	☐	☐	☐	
Trees, plants, shrubs	☐	☐	☐	
Garden produce	☐	☐	☐	
Barbecue	☐	☐	☐	
Outdoor heater	☐	☐	☐	
Stock of oil/solid fuel/gas	☐	☐	☐	
Outside lights	☐	☐	☐	
Water butts	☐	☐	☐	
Clothes line/rotary line	☐	☐	☐	
Dustbins	☐	☐	☐	
Other (please state which)				
	☐	☐	☐	
	☐	☐	☐	
	☐	☐	☐	
	☐	☐	☐	

www.hips.lawsociety.org.uk

Fittings and contents form **TA10**

8 Curtains and blinds

	Included	Excluded	None	Comments
Curtain fittings				
Curtain rails	☐	☐	☐	
Curtain poles	☐	☐	☐	
Pelmets	☐	☐	☐	
Curtains (including net curtains and blinds)				
Bedroom 1	☐	☐	☐	
Bedroom 2	☐	☐	☐	
Bedroom 3	☐	☐	☐	
Bedroom 4	☐	☐	☐	
Bathroom	☐	☐	☐	
Living room	☐	☐	☐	
Dining room	☐	☐	☐	
Kitchen	☐	☐	☐	
Other rooms (please state which)				
	☐	☐	☐	
	☐	☐	☐	
	☐	☐	☐	
	☐	☐	☐	

9 Carpets

	Included	Excluded	None	Comments
Bedroom 1	☐	☐	☐	
Bedroom 2	☐	☐	☐	
Bedroom 3	☐	☐	☐	
Bedroom 4	☐	☐	☐	
Landing	☐	☐	☐	

	Included	Excluded	None	Comments
Stairway	☐	☐	☐	
Hall	☐	☐	☐	
Living room	☐	☐	☐	
Dining room	☐	☐	☐	
Bathroom	☐	☐	☐	
Other rooms (please state which)				
	☐	☐	☐	
	☐	☐	☐	
	☐	☐	☐	
	☐	☐	☐	

10 Other floor coverings

	Included	Excluded	None	Comments
All floor coverings excluding carpets	☐	☐	☐	

11 Kitchen fitments

	Included	Excluded	None	Comments
Fitted cupboards	☐	☐	☐	
Fitted shelves	☐	☐	☐	
Sink	☐	☐	☐	
Fitted oven and grills	☐	☐	☐	
Fitted microwave oven	☐	☐	☐	
Hob(s)	☐	☐	☐	
Extractor hood(s)	☐	☐	☐	

11 Kitchen fitments (continued)

	Included	Excluded	None	Comments
Fitted hooks and racks	☐	☐	☐	
Storage units in kitchen	☐	☐	☐	
Other fitted items (please state which)				
	☐	☐	☐	
	☐	☐	☐	
	☐	☐	☐	
	☐	☐	☐	

12 Other non-fitted appliances

	Included	Excluded	None	Comments
Refrigerator	☐	☐	☐	
Freezer	☐	☐	☐	
Fridge-freezer	☐	☐	☐	
Cooker	☐	☐	☐	
Microwave oven	☐	☐	☐	
Dishwasher	☐	☐	☐	
Washing machine	☐	☐	☐	
Tumble dryer	☐	☐	☐	
Other non-fitted appliances (please state which)				
	☐	☐	☐	
	☐	☐	☐	
	☐	☐	☐	
	☐	☐	☐	

	Included	Excluded	None	Comments
Bath	☐	☐	☐	
Shower fitting for bath	☐	☐	☐	
Toilet	☐	☐	☐	
Hand basin(s)	☐	☐	☐	
Taps	☐	☐	☐	
Plugs	☐	☐	☐	
Mirror	☐	☐	☐	
Cabinets	☐	☐	☐	
Separate shower fittings	☐	☐	☐	
Fitted shelves	☐	☐	☐	
Fitted cupboards	☐	☐	☐	
Towel rail	☐	☐	☐	
Soap and toothbrush holders	☐	☐	☐	
Toilet roll holders	☐	☐	☐	
Other fitted items (please state which)				
	☐	☐	☐	
	☐	☐	☐	
	☐	☐	☐	
	☐	☐	☐	

	Included	Excluded	None	Comments
Fitted wardrobes	☐	☐	☐	
Fitted cupboards	☐	☐	☐	
Fitted shelving	☐	☐	☐	
Cupboards	☐	☐	☐	
Fitted units	☐	☐	☐	
Wall mirrors	☐	☐	☐	
Other items (please state which)				
	☐	☐	☐	
	☐	☐	☐	
	☐	☐	☐	
	☐	☐	☐	

Note: If you are removing any fixtures or fittings you must make good any damage caused. You are also responsible for removing your possessions, including rubbish, from the property, the garage, the garden and any outbuildings or sheds.

The information in this form has been given by:

Name

The Law Society

Page 8 of 8

This form is part of the Law Society's TransAction scheme.
The Law Society is the representative body for solicitors in England and Wales.

© Law Society 2007

Property information form

Document date

Address of the property

Postcode

This form should be completed and read in conjunction with the explanatory notes available separately

1 Boundaries

1.1 Looking towards the property from the road, who either owns or accepts responsibility for the boundary:

(a) on the left?
- [ ] the seller
- [ ] shared
- [ ] next door
- [ ] not known

(b) on the right?
- [ ] the seller
- [ ] shared
- [ ] next door
- [ ] not known

(c) across the back?
- [ ] the seller
- [ ] shared
- [ ] next door
- [ ] not known

(d) across the front?
- [ ] the seller
- [ ] shared
- [ ] next door
- [ ] not known

If the answer is 'not known', please give details of the boundaries that the seller has actually repaired or maintained:

Note: 'boundaries' mean any fence, wall, hedge or ditch which marks the edge of the property.

The Law Society

www.hips.lawsociety.org.uk

TA6

© Law Society 2007
Peapod Solutions Ltd

1.2 Does the seller know of any boundary being moved in the last 20 years?

☐ Yes ☐ No

If Yes, please give details:

> [blank box]

2 Disputes and complaints

2.1 Does the seller know of any dispute or anything which might lead to a dispute about this property or any neighbouring property?

☐ Yes ☐ No

If Yes, please give details:

> [blank box]

2.2 Has the seller made any complaint to any neighbour about what the neighbour has or has not done?

☐ Yes ☐ No

If Yes, please give details:

> [blank box]

2.3 Has the seller received any complaint about anything the seller has, or has not done as owner?

☐ Yes ☐ No

If Yes, please give details:

> [blank box]

3 Notices

3.1 Has the seller either sent or received any communication or notices which in any way affect the property or the neighbouring property (for example, from or to neighbours, the council or a government department)?

☐ Yes ☐ No ☐ Enclosed
☐ To follow ☐ Lost

If Yes, please supply a copy.

3.2 Has the seller had any negotiations or discussions with any neighbour or any local or other authority affecting the property in any way?

☐ Yes ☐ No

If Yes, please give details:

---

4 Guarantees

Are there any guarantees, warranties or insurance policies relating to the property?

☐ Yes ☐ No

If Yes, please give details:

---

5 Utilities

Please indicate which of the following services are connected to or at the property:

☐ Electricity
☐ Gas
☐ Mains drainage
☐ Mains water
☐ Private drains
☐ Private water
☐ Septic tank/Cesspit
☐ Telephone

---

6 Council tax

Please state the council tax band and the amount payable.

Band A - H _____

Amount : £ _____ yearly

Note: Improvements that have already been made can increase the amount of council tax payable following a sale. It is the event of the sale in these circumstances that may cause the council tax banding to be increased. For further information please see the Valuation Office Agency website www.voa.gov.uk

Page 3 of 6

7.1 Is the seller aware of any responsibility to contribute to
the cost of anything in joint use, such as the repair of a
shared drive, boundary or drain?

☐ Yes ☐ No

If Yes, please give details:

7.2 Does the seller contribute to the cost of repair
of anything used by the neighbours, such as the
maintenance of a private road?

☐ Yes ☐ No

If Yes, please give details and state who is responsible
for organising the work and collecting contributions:

8 Arrangements

8.1 Are there any formal or informal arrangements which
the seller has over any neighbouring property?

☐ Yes ☐ No

If Yes, please give details:

8.2 Are there any formal or informal arrangements which
someone else has over the property?

☐ Yes ☐ No

If Yes, please give details:

9.1 Have any of the following changes been made to the whole or any part of the property (including the garden)?

If Yes, in what year were they made?

(a) Building works (including loft conversions, extensions and conservatories)   ☐ Yes   ☐ No   [_____] Year

(b) Change of use   ☐ Yes   ☐ No   [_____] Year

(c) Sub-division   ☐ Yes   ☐ No   [_____] Year

(d) Conversion   ☐ Yes   ☐ No   [_____] Year

(e) Installation of replacement windows, roof windows, glazed doors   ☐ Yes   ☐ No   [_____] Year

(f) Installation of central heating boiler   ☐ Yes   ☐ No   [_____] Year

(g) Installation of solar panels   ☐ Yes   ☐ No   [_____] Year

9.2 If any of the changes listed in 9.1 (a) to (g) above have been made, was planning permission, building regulation approval or listed building consent obtained?

If Yes, please supply copies of the relevant permissions and, where appropriate, certificates of completion.

(a) Building works (including loft conversions, extensions and conservatories)   ☐ Yes   ☐ No   ☐ Enclosed   ☐ To follow   ☐ Lost

(b) Change of use   ☐ Yes   ☐ No   ☐ Enclosed   ☐ To follow   ☐ Lost

(c) Sub-division   ☐ Yes   ☐ No   ☐ Enclosed   ☐ To follow   ☐ Lost

(d) Conversion   ☐ Yes   ☐ No   ☐ Enclosed   ☐ To follow   ☐ Lost

(e) Installation of replacement windows, roof windows, glazed doors   ☐ Yes   ☐ No   ☐ Enclosed   ☐ To follow   ☐ Lost

(f) Installation of central heating boiler   ☐ Yes   ☐ No   ☐ Enclosed   ☐ To follow   ☐ Lost

(g) Installation of solar panels   ☐ Yes   ☐ No   ☐ Enclosed   ☐ To follow   ☐ Lost

9.3 What consents were obtained under any restrictions in
the title registers or any other documents?

Note: The title registers of some properties include clauses which are called 'restrictive covenants'. These may, for example, forbid the owner of the property from carrying out building work unless someone else (often a builder of the house) gives consent.

9.4 Has the property been used other than as a private home in the last 10 years? ☐ Yes ☐ No

If Yes, please give details:

9.5 Has the property been designated as a Listed Building? ☐ Yes ☐ No ☐ Not known

If Yes, please state the year it was designated as a Listed Building. In the year [_____]

9.6 Is the property located in a Conservation Area? ☐ Yes ☐ No ☐ Not known

If Yes, please state the year it was included in the Conservation Area. In the year [_____]

10 Expenses

Has the seller ever incurred any expenses for the use of the property or any of its amenities? ☐ Yes ☐ No

If Yes, please give details:

Note: Ignore mortgage payments, council tax, water rates, and gas, electricity and telephone bills. Disclose anything else, such as the clearance of cesspit or septic tank or drainage rates.

The information in this form has been given by:

Name

Additional property information

Document date [⬚⬚ / ⬚⬚ / ⬚⬚⬚⬚]

**Address or
proposed address
of the property**

Postcode ⬚⬚⬚⬚⬚⬚⬚   Plot number (⬚⬚⬚⬚⬚⬚⬚)

This form should be completed and read in conjunction with the explanatory notes available separately

Part A – Property information

1 Information supplied previously

If this form is being completed to be included in a Home Information Pack - **Go to question 2.**

1.1 Is there a Home Information Pack for the property?   ☐ Yes   ☐ No

If Yes, please give the date of the most recent
Pack and supply a copy.

⬚⬚ / ⬚⬚ / ⬚⬚

☐ Enclosed   ☐ To follow

If No, please explain why:

The Law Society

www.hips.lawsociety.org.uk

TA11

© Law Society 2007
Peapod Solutions Ltd

1.2 Has there been any change in any information given previously (including changes to the TransAction forms and to documents in the Home Information Pack)?

☐ Yes ☐ No

If Yes, please give full details of any change with the name of the form/document and the question number, or supply a copy of the page of the form/document with the changes clearly marked and dated.

☐ Given below ☐ Enclosed

---

2 Services crossing the property or neighbouring property (easements)

2.1 Do any drains, pipes or wires serving the property cross any neighbour's property?

☐ Yes ☐ No ☐ Not known

2.2 Do any drains, pipes or wires leading to any neighbour's property cross the property?

☐ Yes ☐ No ☐ Not known

2.3 Is there any agreement or arrangement about any of these drains, pipes or wires?

☐ Yes ☐ No ☐ Enclosed
☐ To follow

If Yes, please give details or supply a copy.

---

3 Neighbouring land

3.1 Does the seller need to enter any neighbouring land to repair or decorate the building or to maintain any of the boundaries, drains, pipes, wires or other services?

☐ Yes ☐ No

If Yes, please give details:

If No, – **Go to question 3.4.**

3.2 Has the seller always been able to enter any neighbouring land for the reasons given in question 3.1 without objection by the neighbours?

☐ Yes   ☐ No

If No, please give details of any objection:

[ ]

3.3 Has anyone taken steps to stop, complain about, or demand payment for such access being exercised?

☐ Yes   ☐ No

If Yes, please give details, including any sums paid or owing, and if they are paid on a regular basis or only when access is required.

[ ]

3.4 Do any of the seller's neighbours need to enter the seller's land (on which the property is situate) to repair or decorate their building or maintain their boundaries or any drains, pipes or wires?

☐ Yes   ☐ No

If Yes, please give details:

[ ]

3.5 Has the seller ever objected to a neighbour entering the seller's land for the purposes given in 3.4?

☐ Yes   ☐ No

If Yes, please give details:

[ ]

Additional property information TA11

4.1 Is access obtained to any part of the property over private land, common land or a neighbour's land?

☐ Yes ☐ No

If Yes, please give details:

If Yes, please give details:

4.2 Has anyone taken steps to stop, complain about or demand payment for such access being exercised?

☐ Yes ☐ No

If Yes, please give details:

5.1 Does the property benefit from any of the following guarantees, warranties and insurance policies?

If Yes, please supply a copy.

(a) New home warranty (e.g. NHBC)	☐ Yes ☐ No ☐ Enclosed ☐ Lost
(b) Damp	☐ Yes ☐ No ☐ Enclosed ☐ Lost
(c) Double glazing, roof lights, roof windows, glazed doors	☐ Yes ☐ No ☐ Enclosed ☐ Lost
(d) Electrical work	☐ Yes ☐ No ☐ Enclosed ☐ Lost
(e) Roofing	☐ Yes ☐ No ☐ Enclosed ☐ Lost
(f) Timber infestation	☐ Yes ☐ No ☐ Enclosed ☐ Lost
(g) Central heating	☐ Yes ☐ No ☐ Enclosed ☐ Lost
(h) Underpinning	☐ Yes ☐ No ☐ Enclosed ☐ Lost
(i) Other (please state which)	☐ Yes ☐ No ☐ Enclosed ☐ Lost

5.2 Do you have written details of the work done to obtain any of the guarantees, warranties and insurance policies for the items in (a) – (i) above?

If Yes, please supply a copy.

☐ Yes ☐ No
☐ Enclosed ☐ To follow

5.3 Have you made or considered making claims under any of the guarantees, warranties and insurance policies for the items in (a) – (i) above?

☐ Yes   ☐ No

If Yes, please give details:

6 Building control and consents

Note: Improvements or building works that have been carried out since the property was last valued can increase the amount of council tax payable immediately following a sale.

6.1 Have any of the following taken place to the whole or any part of the property (including the garden) and if so, in what year?

(a) Building works (including loft conversions, extensions and conservatories)	☐ Yes	☐ No	Year
(b) Change of use	☐ Yes	☐ No	Year
(c) Sub-division	☐ Yes	☐ No	Year
(d) Conversion	☐ Yes	☐ No	Year
(e) Business activities	☐ Yes	☐ No	Year
(f) Installation of replacement windows, roof lights, roof windows, glazed doors	☐ Yes	☐ No	Year
(g) Installation of central heating boiler	☐ Yes	☐ No	Year
(h) Installation of solar panels	☐ Yes	☐ No	Year

Note: The title registers of some properties include clauses which are called 'restrictive covenants'. These may, for example, forbid the owner of the property from carrying out building work, from using it for business purposes, or from parking a caravan or boat on it unless someone else (often the builder of the house) gives consent.

6.2 Has consent under any restrictions in the title registers or any other documents been obtained for works or activities carried out at the property?

☐ Yes ☐ No ☐ Enclosed
☐ Given below ☐ To follow

If Yes, please give details:

[blank box]

If No, and consent was required, please give details and answer questions (a) – (c) below:

[blank box]

(a) Why was consent not obtained?

[blank box]

(b) From whom should consent have been obtained?

[blank box]

(c) Is there an indemnity policy in place of any missing consent?

[blank box]

Note: If consent should have been obtained under the restrictions and there is no evidence that it was obtained or there has been some problem with the title to the property or its rights, or a missing planning permission, building regulations approval or completion certificate, it is sometimes necessary to take out an indemnity policy to protect the owner of the property and the lender against a future claim.

6.3 Have replacement windows, or roof lights, or roof windows or glazed doors been installed **and** the work completed on or after 1 April 2002?

☐ Yes ☐ No ☐ Enclosed
☐ To follow ☐ Lost

If Yes, please supply either a FENSA certificate or a building regulation certificate.

Additional property information TA11

If this form is being completed to be put in the Home Information Pack question 7 should **not be** answered at this stage.

Is there any indemnity policy for the property in relation to any matter, other than a policy for missing consents or documents? (For example, defective title, chancel repair, maisonette indemnity policy).

☐ Yes   ☐ No   ☐ Enclosed

☐ To follow

If Yes, please give a list below and supply a copy of each policy.

8 Party walls

Has any notice been received under The Party Wall Act 1996 in respect of any shared/party boundaries?

☐ Yes   ☐ No   ☐ Enclosed

☐ To follow

If Yes, please supply a copy and give details of any works carried out or agreed.

9 Occupiers

9.1 Does anyone other than the seller live at the property?

☐ Yes   ☐ No

If No, – **Go to question 10.**

9.2 Please state the age of those occupiers under the age of 18.

9.3 Does the seller believe that any of these occupiers have the right to stay on the property without the seller's permission?

☐ Yes ☐ No

If Yes, please give details:

Note: These rights may have arisen without the seller realising. For example, rights may arise when occupiers have paid towards the cost of buying the property, paid for improvements or helped make mortgage payments. This is a matter on which the seller may need to take legal advice.

9.4 Are any of the occupiers tenants or lodgers?

☐ Yes ☐ No ☐ Enclosed ☐ To follow

If Yes, please give details and supply a copy of any Tenancy Agreement.

If this form is being completed to be put in the Home Information Pack question 9.5 should **not** be answered at this stage.

9.5 Have all the occupiers agreed to sign the contract for sale agreeing to leave by the completion date?

☐ Yes ☐ No

If Yes, please state their full name(s):

If No, please give details:

Additional property information TA11

10 Dealings within the last five years

10.1 Have there been any transfers of the whole or part of the property in the last five years?

☐ Yes ☐ No

If Yes, were these transfers of the property:

(a) for full market value

☐ Yes ☐ No

(b) by way of gift

☐ Yes ☐ No

10.2 If Yes to any part of 10.1, please give details:

11 Services

11.1 Please confirm that all meters will be read upon completion and that the seller will not apply for any of the services to be disconnected up to or on completion without prior reference to the buyer.

☐ Yes ☐ No

If No, please give details:

11.2 Have there been difficulties regarding connection of any services and/or any recurrent difficulties with the provision of services to the property?

☐ Yes ☐ No

If Yes, please give details:

Part B – Service supplier information

1 Cable/Satellite

1.1 Is there a cable/satellite service to the property? ☐ Yes ☐ No

If Yes, please state which. ☐ Cable ☐ Satellite

1.2 Is any cable/satellite equipment included in the sale? ☐ Yes ☐ No

If Yes, please give details:

2 Electricity

2.1 Has the property been rewired in whole or part during the seller's ownership? ☐ Yes ☐ No

If Yes, please state the date the work was carried out. ☐☐ / ☐☐ / ☐☐

2.2 When was the whole or part of the electrical installation last tested and approved by a qualified and registered electrician? ☐☐ / ☐☐ / ☐☐

2.3 Has any electrical work been carried out to the property since 1 January 2005 which requires notification under Part P (Electrical Safety) of the Building Regulations? ☐ Yes ☐ No

If Yes, please supply the following:

(a) a copy of the signed BS7671 Electrical Safety Certificate for all those types of electrical work that have been carried out

☐ Enclosed ☐ With deeds ☐ To follow ☐ Lost

and

(b) in the case of a registered installer, the installers Building Regulations compliance certificate or, in the case of an unregistered installer, the Building Contract Departments completion certificate.

☐ Enclosed ☐ With deeds ☐ To follow ☐ Lost

www.hips.lawsociety.org.uk

Additional property information TA11

3.1 Is there a central heating system at the property? ☐ Yes ☐ No

If No, **Go to question 3.7.**

3.2 What type of central heating system is at the property? ☐ Gas ☐ Oil

3.3 When was the central heating system installed?

In the year ⬭

☐ Not known

3.4 Is the central heating system in good working order? ☐ Yes ☐ No

3.5 Has repair and/or maintenance work to the central heating system been carried out during the seller's ownership of the property? ☐ Yes ☐ No

If Yes, please give a summary including the date of the last service:

☐ ☐ / ☐ ☐ / ☐ ☐ Last service

3.6 Have any central heating boilers or water tanks been installed at the property on or after 1 April 2002? ☐ Yes ☐ No

If Yes, please supply the following:

(a) the installation date

☐ ☐ / ☐ ☐ / ☐ ☐

(b) a copy of the appropriate compliance certificate from the installer

☐ Enclosed ☐ With deeds

☐ To follow ☐ Lost

(c) copies of the appropriate building regulations approvals and building regulations completion certificate.

☐ Enclosed ☐ With deeds

☐ To follow ☐ Lost

Note: The appropriate compliance certificate from the installer in 3.6(b) must confirm that the installer is a member of OFTEX, or HETAS, or CORGI. It must also state that the works comply with the building regulations and must include the installer's confirmation that the original certificate has been lodged with the local authority.

3.7 Are there any oil fired heaters at the property? ☐ Yes ☐ No

If Yes, does the seller intend to sell any surplus oil to the buyer and if so, at what price? ☐ Yes ☐ No

£ _____

3.8 Is any water heating apparatus, separate from a central heating system, in good working order? ☐ Yes ☐ No ☐ Not known

4 Telephone and broadband

4.1 Does the seller intend to continue to use the current telephone number? ☐ Yes ☐ No

If No, please state the telephone number:

☐☐☐☐☐☐☐☐☐☐☐☐

4.2 Does the seller have a broadband internet connection via a BT telephone line? ☐ Yes ☐ No

5 Television

5.1 Is there a television aerial? ☐ Yes ☐ No

If Yes, please answer the following:

(a) where is it located?

_____

(b) does it exclusively serve the property? ☐ Yes ☐ No

6 Water

6.1 Please supply a copy of the latest water charge account and the sewerage account (if any). ☐ Enclosed ☐ To follow ☐ Not applicable

6.2 Is the water supply on a meter? ☐ Yes ☐ No

The information in this form has been given by:

Name _____

www.hips.lawsociety.org.uk

Additional property information TA11

Service suppliers

Address or proposed address of the property

Postcode ☐☐☐☐☐☐☐   Plot number

Broadband	
Supplier name	
Address	
Phone number	
Email address	
Reference	

Telephone	
Supplier name	
Address	
Phone number	
Email address	
Reference	

Cable/Satellite

Supplier name	
Address	
Phone number	
Email address	
Reference	

Council Tax

Council	
Address	
Phone number	
Email address	
Reference	

Electricity

Supplier name	
Address	
Phone number	
Email address	
Reference	

Additional property information TA11

Gas

Supplier name	
Address	
Phone number	
Email address	
Reference	

Sewerage

Company	
Address	
Phone number	
Email address	
Reference	

Water and drainage charge

Company	
Address	
Phone number	
Email address	
Reference	

The Law Society

Leasehold information form

Document date ☐☐ / ☐☐ / ☐☐☐☐

Address of the property

Postcode ☐☐☐☐☐☐☐☐

This form should be completed and read in conjunction with the explanatory notes available separately

1 Other leases

1.1 Is there any headlease?

If Yes, please supply a copy.

☐ Yes ☐ No ☐ Enclosed
☐ To follow ☐ Not known

1.2 Is there any underlease?

If Yes, please supply a copy.

☐ Yes ☐ No ☐ Enclosed
☐ To follow ☐ Not known

1.3 In respect of any headlease or underlease of the whole or any part of the property, state any amounts owing or owed by or to the seller relating to rent, service charge, insurance premiums or other financial contribution.

The Law Society

www.hips.lawsociety.org.uk

© Law Society 2007

Peapod Solutions Ltd

2 Management company

2.1 Is there a management company which is run by the tenants? ☐ Yes ☐ No

If Yes, please supply copies of the following:

(a) Memorandum and articles of association ☐ Enclosed ☐ To follow

(b) The share or membership certificate ☐ Enclosed ☐ To follow

(c) The company's accounts for the last three years ☐ Enclosed ☐ To follow

(d) The names and addresses of the secretary and treasurer of the company:

2.2 Has the management company been dissolved or removed from the register at Companies House? ☐ Yes ☐ No

3 Maintenance charges

3.1 Have there been any problems in the last three years between flat owners and the landlord or management company about maintenance charges, or the method of management? ☐ Yes ☐ No

If Yes, please give details:

3.2 Has there been any challenge to the maintenance charges or any expense in the last three years? ☐ Yes ☐ No

If Yes, please give details:

3.3 Has the landlord had any problems with collecting the maintenance charges from other flat owners?　　☐ Yes　☐ No

If Yes, please give details:

>

4.1 Has a notice been received from any landlord or landlord's agent?

☐ Yes　☐ No　☐ Enclosed
☐ To follow

If Yes, please supply a copy.

4.2 Has any other notice been received from any other person or authority?

☐ Yes　☐ No　☐ Enclosed
☐ To follow

If Yes, please supply a copy.

4.3 Are any changes to the terms of the lease proposed or has the landlord given any consents under the lease? (This could be in a formal document, a letter or even oral).

☐ Yes　☐ No　☐ Enclosed
☐ To follow

If Yes, please give details or supply a copy.

>

4.4 Please provide the name and address of the landlord or landlord's agent for service of any notice of change of ownership.

☐ To follow　　☐ Not applicable

>

Note: A notice could be on a printed form or in the form of a letter and a buyer will wish to know if anything of this sort has been received.

5.1 Has the seller received any complaint from the landlord, any other landlord, management company or any other occupier about anything the seller has or has not done?

☐ Yes   ☐ No

If Yes, please give details:

5.2 Has the seller complained or does the seller have cause for complaint to or about the landlord, management company or any other occupier?

☐ Yes   ☐ No

If Yes, please give details:

6   Buildings insurance of the property

6.1 Is the seller responsible under the terms of the lease for arranging the buildings insurance of the property?

☐ Yes   ☐ No

If Yes, please supply copies of:

(a) the insurance policy   ☐ Enclosed   ☐ To follow

(b) the receipt for the last payment of the premium   ☐ Enclosed   ☐ To follow

6.2 Is the landlord or management company responsible for arranging the buildings insurance of the property?

☐ Yes   ☐ No

If Yes, please supply copies of:

(a) the insurance policy   ☐ Enclosed   ☐ To follow

(b) the schedule for the current year   ☐ Enclosed   ☐ To follow

6.3 Do the insurers record the interests of the buyer's mortgagee and the buyer on the policy?

☐ Yes   ☐ No   ☐ Not known

7 Decoration

7.1 When was the outside of the building last decorated? In the year [ ] ☐ Not known

7.2 When were any internal communal parts last decorated? In the year [ ] ☐ Not known

7.3 When was the inside of the property last decorated? In the year [ ] ☐ Not known

8 Alterations

8.1 Is the seller aware of any alterations having been made to the property since the lease was originally granted? ☐ Yes ☐ No ☐ Not known

If Yes, please give details:

[ ]

8.2 If alterations have been made to the property since the lease was originally granted, was the landlord's consent obtained?

☐ Yes ☐ No

☐ Enclosed ☐ To follow

☐ Not known ☐ Not required

If Yes, please supply copies of any consents obtained.

9 Occupation

9.1 Is the seller now occupying the property as their sole or main home? ☐ Yes ☐ No

9.2 Has the seller occupied the property as their sole or main home (apart from usual holidays and business trips):

(a) continuously throughout the last 12 months? ☐ Yes ☐ No

(b) continuously throughout the last three years? ☐ Yes ☐ No

(c) for periods totalling at least three years during the last 10 years? ☐ Yes ☐ No

10.1 Has the seller served on the landlord or any other person a notice under the enfranchisement legislation stating the desire to buy the freehold or be granted an extended lease?

☐ Yes ☐ No ☐ Enclosed ☐ To follow

If Yes, please supply a copy.

10.2 If the property is a flat in a block, is the seller aware of the service of any notice under the enfranchisement legislation relating to the possible collective purchase of the freehold of the block or part of it?

☐ Yes ☐ No ☐ Enclosed ☐ To follow

If Yes, please supply a copy.

10.3 Has the seller received any response to that notice?

☐ Yes ☐ No ☐ Enclosed ☐ To follow

If Yes, please supply a copy.

The information in this form has been given by:

Name (   )

The Law Society

Land Registry
Transfer of whole of registered title(s)

If you need more room than is provided for in a panel, and your software allows, you can expand any panel in the form. Alternatively use continuation sheet CS and attach it to this form.

Leave blank if not yet registered.	**1** Title number(s) of the property:
Insert address including postcode (if any) or other description of the property, for example 'land adjoining 2 Acacia Avenue'.	**2** Property:
	3 Date:
Give full name(s).	**4** Transferor:
Complete as appropriate where the transferor is a company.	For UK incorporated companies/LLPs Registered number of company or limited liability partnership including any prefix: For overseas companies (a) Territory of incorporation: (b) Registered number in England and Wales including any prefix:
Give full name(s).	**5** Transferee for entry in the register:
Complete as appropriate where the transferee is a company. Also, for an overseas company, unless an arrangement with Land Registry exists, lodge either a certificate in Form 7 in Schedule 3 to the Land Registration Rules 2003 or a certified copy of the constitution in English or Welsh, or other evidence permitted by rule 183 of the Land Registration Rules 2003.	For UK incorporated companies/LLPs Registered number of company or limited liability partnership including any prefix: For overseas companies (a) Territory of incorporation: (b) Registered number in England and Wales including any prefix:
Each transferee may give up to three addresses for service, one of which must be a postal address whether or not in the UK (including the postcode, if any). The others can be any combination of a postal address, a UK DX box number or an electronic address.	**6** Transferee's intended address(es) for service for entry in the register:
	7 The transferor transfers the property to the transferee

Place 'X' in the appropriate box. State the currency unit if other than sterling. If none of the boxes apply, insert an appropriate memorandum in panel 11.

8 Consideration

☐ The transferor has received from the transferee for the property the following sum (in words and figures):

£

☐ The transfer is not for money or anything that has a monetary value

☐ Insert other receipt as appropriate:

Place 'X' in any box that applies.

Add any modifications.

9 The transferor transfers with

☐ full title guarantee

☐ limited title guarantee

Where the transferee is more than one person, place 'X' in the appropriate box.

10 Declaration of trust. The transferee is more than one person and

☐ they are to hold the property on trust for themselves as joint tenants

☐ they are to hold the property on trust for themselves as tenants in common in equal shares

Complete as necessary.

☐ they are to hold the property on trust:

Insert here any required or permitted statement, certificate or application and any agreed covenants, declarations and so on.

11 Additional provisions

The transferor must execute this transfer as a deed using the space opposite. If there is more than one transferor, all must execute. Forms of execution are given in Schedule 9 to the Land Registration Rules 2003. If the transfer contains transferee's covenants or declarations or contains an application by the transferee (such as for a restriction), it must also be executed by the transferee.

12   Execution

Land Registry
Transfer of part of registered title(s)

If you need more room than is provided for in a panel, and your software allows, you can expand any panel in the form. Alternatively use continuation sheet CS and attach it to this form.

Leave blank if not yet registered.	**1** Title number(s) out of which the property is transferred:
When application for registration is made these title number(s) should be entered in panel 2 of Form AP1.	**2** Other title number(s) against which matters contained in this transfer are to be registered or noted, if any:
Insert address, including postcode (if any), or other description of the property transferred. Any physical exclusions, such as mines and minerals, should be defined.	**3** Property:
Place 'X' in the appropriate box and complete the statement.	The property is identified
For example 'edged red'.	☐ on the attached plan and shown:
For example 'edged and numbered 1 in blue'.	☐ on the title plan(s) of the above titles and shown:
Any plan lodged must be signed by the transferor.	
	4 Date:
Give full name(s).	**5** Transferor:
Complete as appropriate where the transferor is a company.	**For UK incorporated companies/LLPs** Registered number of company or limited liability partnership including any prefix:
	For overseas companies (a) Territory of incorporation:
	(b) Registered number in England and Wales including any prefix:
Give full name(s).	**6** Transferee for entry in the register:
	For UK incorporated companies/LLPs Registered number of company or limited liability partnership including any prefix:
Complete as appropriate where the transferee is a company. Also, for an overseas company, unless an arrangement with Land Registry exists, lodge either a certificate in Form 7 in Schedule 3 to the Land Registration Rules 2003 or a certified copy of the constitution in English or Welsh, or other evidence permitted by rule 183 of the Land Registration Rules 2003.	**For overseas companies** (a) Territory of incorporation: (b) Registered number in England and Wales including any prefix:
Each transferee may give up to three addresses for service, one of which must be a postal address whether or not in the UK (including the postcode, if any). The others can be any combination of a postal address, a UK DX box number or an electronic address.	**7** Transferee's intended address(es) for service for entry in the register:

	8	The transferor transfers the property to the transferee

Place 'X' in the appropriate box. State the currency unit if other than sterling. If none of the boxes apply, insert an appropriate memorandum in panel 12.

9 Consideration

☐ The transferor has received from the transferee for the property the following sum (in words and figures):

☐ The transfer is not for money or anything that has a monetary value

☐ Insert other receipt as appropriate:

Place 'X' in any box that applies.

Add any modifications.

10 The transferor transfers with

☐ full title guarantee

☐ limited title guarantee

Where the transferee is more than one person, place 'X' in the appropriate box.

11 Declaration of trust. The transferee is more than one person and

☐ they are to hold the property on trust for themselves as joint tenants

☐ they are to hold the property on trust for themselves as tenants in common in equal shares

Complete as necessary.

☐ they are to hold the property on trust:

Use this panel for:
- definitions of terms not defined above
- rights granted or reserved
- restrictive covenants
- other covenants
- agreements and declarations
- any required or permitted statements
- other agreed provisions.

The prescribed subheadings may be added to, amended, repositioned or omitted.

Any other land affected by rights granted or reserved or by restrictive covenants should be defined by reference to a plan.

Any other land affected should be defined by reference to a plan and the title numbers referred to in panel 2.

12 Additional provisions

Definitions

Rights granted for the benefit of the property

Any other land affected should be defined by reference to a plan and the title numbers referred to in panel 2.

Rights reserved for the benefit of other land

Include words of covenant.

Restrictive covenants by the Transferee

Include words of covenant.

Restrictive covenants by the Transferor

Insert here any required or permitted statements, certificates or applications and any agreed declarations and so on.

Other

The transferor must execute this transfer as a deed using the space opposite. If there is more than one transferor, all must execute. Forms of execution are given in Schedule 9 to the Land Registration Rules 2003. If the transfer contains transferee's covenants or declarations or contains an application by the transferee (such as for a restriction), it must also be executed by the transferee.

13   Execution

Land Registry
Application by purchaser for official search with priority of the whole of the land in a registered title or a pending first registration application

OS1

\

Use one form per title.

If you need more room than is provided for in a panel, and your software allows, you can expand any panel in the form. Alternatively use continuation sheet CS and attach it to this form.

Land Registry is unable to give legal advice but our website www1.landregistry.gov.uk provides guidance on Land Registry applications. This includes public guides and practice guides (aimed at conveyancers) that can also be obtained from any Land Registry office.

See www1.landregistry.gov.uk/regional if you are unsure which Land Registry office to send this application to.

'Conveyancer' is a term used in this form. It is defined in rule 217(1) of the Land Registration Rules 2003 and includes, among others, solicitor, licensed conveyancer and fellow of the Institute of Legal Executives.

LAND REGISTRY USE ONLY
Record of fees paid
Particulars of under/over payments
Reference number
Fees debited £

Where there is more than one local authority serving an area, enter the one to which council tax or business rates are normally paid.	1	Local authority serving the property:
Enter the title number of the registered estate or that allotted to the pending first registration.	2	Title number of the property:
Insert address including postcode (if any) or other description of the property, for example 'land adjoining 2 Acacia Avenue'.	3	Property:
Enter the full names. If there are more than two persons, enter the first two only.	4	Registered proprietor/Applicant for first registration SURNAME/COMPANY NAME: FORENAME(S): SURNAME/COMPANY NAME: FORENAME(S):

	4	Application and fee	
See fees calculator at www1.landregistry.gov.uk/fees		**Application**	**Fee paid (£)**
		Official search of whole with priority	

Fee payment method

Place 'X' in the appropriate box.

The fee will be charged to the account specified in panel 6.

☐ cheque made payable to 'Land Registry'
☐ Land Registry credit account
☐ direct debit, under an agreement with Land Registry

If you are paying by credit account or direct debit, this will be the account charged.	**6** This application is sent to Land Registry by Key number (if applicable): Name: Address or UK DX box number: Email address: Reference: Phone no: Fax no:

Place 'X' in one box only.

For a search of a registered title enter a date falling within the definition of 'search from date' in rule 131 of the Land Registration Rules 2003. If the date entered is not such a date the application may be rejected.

7   Application and search from date

☐   I apply for a search of the individual register of a registered title to ascertain whether any adverse entry has been made in the register or day list since [   ]

☒   I apply for a search in relation to a pending application for first registration to ascertain whether any adverse entry has been made in the day list since the date of the pending first registration application.

Provide the full name(s) of each purchaser or lessee or chargee.

8   The applicant:

9   Reason for application

Place 'X' in one box only.

I certify that the applicant intends to

☐   **P**urchase

☒   take a **L**ease

☐   take a registered **C**harge

If a conveyancer is acting for the applicant, that conveyancer must sign. If no conveyancer is acting, the applicant (if more than one person then each) must sign.

10

      Signature of applicant
      or their conveyancer: ---

      Date:

WARNING
If you dishonestly enter information or make a statement that you know is, or might be, untrue or misleading, and intend by doing so to make a gain for yourself or another person, or to cause loss or the risk of loss to another person, you may commit the offence of fraud under section 1 of the Fraud Act 2006, the maximum penalty for which is 10 years' imprisonment or an unlimited fine, or both.

Failure to complete this form with proper care may result in a loss of protection under the Land Registration Act 2002 if, as a result, a mistake is made in the register.

Under section 66 of the Land Registration Act 2002 most documents (including this form) kept by the registrar relating to an application to the registrar or referred to in the register are open to public inspection and copying. If you believe a document contains prejudicial information, you may apply for that part of the document to be made exempt using Form EX1, under rule 136 of the Land Registration Rules 2003.

© Crown copyright (ref: LR/HO) 07/08

Land Registry
Application by purchaser for official search with priority of part of the land in a registered title or a pending first registration application

OS2

Use one form per title.

If you need more room than is provided for in a panel, and your software allows, you can expand any panel in the form. Alternatively use continuation sheet CS and attach it to this form.

Land Registry is unable to give legal advice but our website www1.landregistry.gov.uk provides guidance on Land Registry applications. This includes public guides and practice guides (aimed at conveyancers) that can also be obtained from any Land Registry office.

See www1.landregistry.gov.uk/regional if you are unsure which Land Registry office to send this application to.

'Conveyancer' is a term used in this form. It is defined in rule 217(1) of the Land Registration Rules 2003 and includes, among others, solicitor, licensed conveyancer and fellow of the Institute of Legal Executives.

LAND REGISTRY USE ONLY
Record of fees paid
Particulars of under/over payments
Reference number
Fees debited £

Where there is more than one local authority serving an area, enter the one to which council tax or business rates are normally paid.

1   Local authority serving the property:

Enter the title number of the registered estate or that allotted to the pending first registration.

2   Title number:

Enter the full names. If there are more than two persons, enter the first two only.

3   Registered proprietor/Applicant for first registration

SURNAME/COMPANY NAME:

FORENAME(S):

SURNAME/COMPANY NAME:

FORENAME(S):

4   Application and fee

Application	Fee paid (£)
Official search of part with priority	

See fees calculator at www1.landregistry.gov.uk/fees

Place 'X' in the appropriate box.

The fee will be charged to the account specified in panel 5.

Fee payment method
- ☐ cheque made payable to 'Land Registry'
- ☐ Land Registry credit account
- ☐ direct debit, under an agreement with Land Registry

If you are paying by credit account or direct debit, this will be the account charged.	**5** This application is sent to Land Registry by Key number (if applicable): Name: Address or UK DX box number: Email address: Reference: Phone no: Fax no:

Insert address including postcode (if any) or other description of the property, for example 'land adjoining 2 Acacia Avenue'.	**6** Property to be searched:
	
	(a) Where an estate plan has been approved
	      (i) the plot number(s) is/are
	      (ii) the date of approval of the estate plan is
	
	      OR

A plan must be attached when (b) is completed.	(b) The property is shown
	      on the attached plan.
	      OR

Insert title number.	(c) The property is shown on the title plan of
Provide the full name(s) of each purchaser or lessee or chargee.	**7** The applicant:
Place 'X' in one box only. For a search of a registered title enter a date falling within the definition of 'search from date' in rule 131 of the Land Registration Rules 2003. If the date entered is not such a date the application may be rejected.	**8** Application and search from date ☐ I apply for a search of the individual register of a registered title to ascertain whether any adverse entry has been made in the register or day list since ☐ I apply for a search in relation to a pending application for first registration to ascertain whether any adverse entry has been made in the day list since the date of the pending first registration application.
Place 'X' in the appropriate box.	**9** Reason for application I certify that the applicant intends to ☐ **P**urchase ☐ take a **L**ease ☐ take a registered **C**harge
If a conveyancer is acting for the applicant, that conveyancer must sign. If no conveyancer is acting, the applicant (if more than one person then each) must sign.	**10** Signature of applicant or their conveyancer: ------------------------------------ Date:

WARNING
If you dishonestly enter information or make a statement that you know is, or might be, untrue or misleading, and intend by doing so to make a gain for yourself or another person, or to cause loss or the risk of loss to another person, you may commit the offence of fraud under section 1 of the Fraud Act 2006, the maximum penalty for which is 10 years' imprisonment or an unlimited fine, or both.

Failure to complete this form with proper care may result in a loss of protection under the Land Registration Act 2002 if, as a result, a mistake is made in the register.

Land Registry
Cancellation of entries relating to a registered charge

This form should be accompanied by either Form AP1 or Form DS2

If you need more room than is provided for in a panel, and your software allows, you can expand any panel in the form. Alternatively use continuation sheet CS and attach it to this form.

	1 Title number(s) of the property:
Insert address including postcode (if any) or other description of the property, for example 'land adjoining 2 Acacia Avenue'.	2 Property:
	3 Date:
Include register entry number, if more than one charge of same date to same lender.	4 Date of charge:
	5 Lender:
Complete as appropriate where the cautioner is a company.	<u>For UK incorporated companies/LLPs</u> Registered number of company or limited liability partnership including any prefix: <u>For overseas companies</u> (a) Territory of incorporation: (b) Registered number in England and Wales including any prefix:
	6 The lender acknowledges that the property identified in panel 2 is no longer charged as security for the payment of sums due under the charge
	7 Date of Land Registry facility letter (if any):
The lender must execute this transfer as a deed using the space opposite. If there is more than one lender, all must execute. Forms of execution are given in Schedule 9 to the Land Registration Rules 2003. Alternatively the lender may sign in accordance with the facility letter referred to in panel 7.	8 Execution

Land Registry
Application for official copies of register/ plan or certificate in Form CI

Use one form per title.

If you need more room than is provided for in a panel, and your software allows, you can expand any panel in the form. Alternatively use continuation sheet CS and attach it to this form.

Land Registry is unable to give legal advice but our website www1.landregistry.gov.uk provides guidance on Land Registry applications. This includes public guides and practice guides (aimed at conveyancers) that can also be obtained from any Land Registry office.

See www1.landregistry.gov.uk/regional if you are unsure which Land Registry office to send this application to.

Where there is more than one local authority serving an area, enter the one to which council tax or business rates are normally paid.

Use a separate form for each registered title.

Place 'X' in the appropriate box.

1	Local authority serving the property:

2 Details of estate

(a) Title number if known:

(b) (Where the title number is unknown) this application relates to

☐ freehold ☐ leasehold ☐ manor

☐ franchise ☐ caution against first registration

☐ rentcharge ☐ profit a prendre in gross

3 Property

Flat/unit number:

Postal number or description:

Name of road:

Name of locality:

Town:

Postcode:

4	Application and fee		
	Application	Total number of all copies or certificates requested in panel 7	Fee paid (£)
	Official copy of register /plan or certificate of inspection of title plan		

Fee payment method

☐ cheque made payable to 'Land Registry'

☐ Land Registry credit account

☐ direct debit, under an agreement with Land Registry

---

5 This application is sent to Land Registry by

Key number (if applicable):

Name:

Address or UK DX box number:

Email address:

Reference:

Phone no:	Fax no:

---

6 Issue of official copies in paper format where an email address has been supplied

If you have supplied an email address in panel 5, then, unless you complete the box below, any official copy will be issued electronically to that address, if there is a direction under section 100(4) of the Land Registration Act 2002 by the registrar covering such issuing.

☐ I have supplied an email address but require the official copy(ies) to be issued in paper format instead of being issued electronically

---

7 I apply for

_____ official copy(ies) of the register of the above mentioned property

_____ official copy(ies) of the title plan or caution plan of the above mentioned property

_____ certificate(s) of inspection of title plan, in which case either

i. ☐ an estate plan has been approved and the plot number is:

or

ii. ☐ no estate plan has been approved and a certificate is to be issued in respect of the land shown on the attached plan and copy

---

See fees calculator at www1.landregistry.gov.uk/fees

Place 'X' in the appropriate box.

The fee will be charged to the account specified in panel 5.

If you are paying by credit account or direct debit, this will be the account charged.

Please note that the facility of issuing copies electronically is not available at present. When it is, a direction will appear on our website and details will be given in Public Guide 1 and Practice Guide 11. Until there is a direction, you do not need to complete this panel to obtain an official copy in paper format.

Official copies issued electronically are in 'Portable Document Format' (PDF) which replicates the appearance of the hard copy version. You will need Adobe Acrobat Reader (which you can install free from www.adobe.com) to open the document.

Place 'X' in the box if applicable.

Indicate how many copies of each are required.

Place 'X' in the appropriate box.

State reference, for example 'edged red'.

Place 'X' in the appropriate box.

8	If an application for registration is pending against the title
	☐ I require an official copy back-dated prior to the receipt of the application
	☐ I require an official copy on completion of that application
9	
	Signature of applicant: _____
	Date:

Land Registry
Application to change the register

LAND REGISTRY USE ONLY
Record of fees paid
Particulars of under/over payments
Reference number
Fees debited £

Where there is more than one local authority serving an area, enter the one to which council tax or business rates are normally paid.

1 Local authority serving the property:
-
Full postcode of property (if any):

Enter the title number of each title that requires an entry to be made in that register.

2 Title number(s) of the property:

Place 'X' in the appropriate box.

Give a brief description of the part affected, for example 'edged red on the plan to the transfer dated ....'.

3 The application affects
☐ the whole of the title(s)
☐ part of the title(s) as shown:

4 Application, priority and fees

Applications in priority order	Price paid/Value (£)	Fees paid (£)
Total fees (£)		

See fees calculator at www1.landregistry.gov.uk/fees

Place 'X' in the appropriate box.

The fee will be charged to the account specified in panel 7.

Fee payment method
☐ cheque made payable to 'Land Registry'
☐ direct debit, under an agreement with Land Registry

Peapod Solutions Ltd.

List the documents lodged with this form. Copy documents should be listed separately. If you supply a certified copy of an original document we will return the original; if a certified copy is not supplied, we may retain the original document and it may be destroyed.	**5** Documents lodged with this form:
Provide the full name(s) of the person(s) applying to change the register. Where a conveyancer lodges the application, this must be the name(s) of the client(s), not the conveyancer. Complete as appropriate where the applicant is a company. Also, for an overseas company, unless an arrangement with Land Registry exists, lodge either a certificate in Form 7 in Schedule 3 to the Land Registration Rules 2003 or a certified copy of the constitution in English or Welsh, or other evidence permitted by rule 183 of the Land Registration Rules 2003.	**6** The applicant: **For UK incorporated companies/LLPs** Registered number of company or limited liability partnership including any prefix: **For overseas companies** (a) Territory of incorporation: (b) Registered number in England and Wales including any prefix:
If you are paying by direct debit, this will be the account charged. This is the address to which we will normally send requisitions and return documents. However if you insert an email address, we will use this whenever possible..	**7** This application is sent to Land Registry by Key number (if applicable): Name: Address or UK DX box number: Email address: Reference: Phone no: Fax no:
Complete this panel if you want us to notify someone else that we have completed this application.	**8** Third party notification Name: Address or UK DX box number: Email address: Reference:
Place 'X' in the appropriate box. In this and panel 10, each proprietor may give up to three addresses for service, one of which must be a postal address whether or not in the UK (including the postcode, if any). The others can be any combination of a postal address, a UK DX box number or an electronic address.	**9** The address(es) for service for each proprietor of the registered estate(s) to be entered in the register is ☐ the address of the property (where this is a single postal address) ☐ the address(es) for service from the transfer/assent ☐ (for existing proprietors who are remaining in the register) the current address(es) for service in the register ☐ the following address(es):

Where a charge has an MD reference we will ignore an address given in this panel unless the charge is in favour of a United Kingdom bank and neither the charge form nor any agreement we have with the lender specifies an address for service.

For permitted addresses see note to panel 9.

Complete as appropriate where the applicant is a company. Also, for an overseas company, unless an arrangement with Land Registry exists, lodge either a certificate in Form 7 in Schedule 3 to the Land Registration Rules 2003 or a certified copy of the constitution in English or Welsh, or other evidence permitted by rule 183 of the Land Registration Rules 2003.

If this statement applies (i) place 'X' in the box and (ii) enclose Form DI.

Section 27 of the Land Registration Act 2002 lists the registrable dispositions.

Rule 57 of the Land Registration Rules 2003 sets out the disclosable overriding interests that you must tell us about.

Full details of the evidence of identity that is required can be found in Practice Guide 67 and in Public Guide 20.

Place 'X' in the appropriate box.

Conveyancer is defined in rule 217(1) of the Land Registration Rules 2003 and includes, among others, solicitor, licensed conveyancer and fellow of the Institute of Legal Executives.

10   Name and address(es) for service of the proprietor of any new charge to be entered in the register:

For UK incorporated companies/LLPs
Registered number of company or limited liability partnership including any prefix:

For overseas companies
(a) Territory of incorporation:

(b) Registered number in England and Wales including any prefix:

11   Disclosable overriding interests

☐   This application relates to a registrable disposition and disclosable overriding interests affect the registered estate.

12   Confirmation of identity

When registering transfers, charges, leases and other dispositions of land, or giving effect to a discharge or release of a registered charge, Land Registry relies on the steps that conveyancers take, where appropriate, to verify the identity of their clients. These checks reduce the risk of property fraud.

Where a person was not represented by a conveyancer, Land Registry requires 'evidence of identity' in respect of that person, except where the first alternative in panel 13(2) applies.

'Evidence of identity' is evidence provided in accordance with any current direction made by the Chief Land Registrar under section 100(4) of the Land Registration Act 2002 for the purpose of confirming a person's identity.

If this application is to register a transfer, lease or charge, or to give effect to a discharge in Form DS1 or a release in Form DS3 complete one of the following

☐   I am a conveyancer, and I have completed panel 13

☐   I am not a conveyancer, and I have completed panel 14

13 Where the application is sent to Land Registry by a conveyancer

(1) Details of conveyancer acting

If you are sending an application to register a transfer, lease or charge, for each party to each disposition that is to be registered state in the table below the details of the conveyancer (if any) who represented them.

Where a party is not represented by a conveyancer you must also complete (2) below.

Place 'X' in the box in the second column if the person or firm who is sending the application to Land Registry represented that party in the transaction. Otherwise complete the details in the third column. If the party is not represented insert 'none' in the third column.

Name of transferor, landlord, transferee, tenant, borrower or lender		Conveyancer's name, address and reference
	☐	
		Reference:
	☐	
		Reference:
	☐	
		Reference:

If you are sending an application to give effect to a discharge in Form DS1 or release in Form DS3 for each lender, state in the table below the details of the conveyancer (if any) who represented them.

Where a lender is not represented by a conveyancer you must also complete (2) below.

Place 'X' in the box in the second column if the person or firm who is sending the application to Land Registry represented that party in the transaction. Otherwise complete the details in the third column. If the party is not represented insert 'none' in the third column.

Name of lender		Conveyancer's name, address and reference
	☐	
		Reference:
	☐	
		Reference:

Place 'X' in the appropriate box(es).

Insert the name of each unrepresented transferor, landlord, transferee, tenant, borrower or lender for whom you give this confirmation.

Evidence of identity is defined in panel 12. Full details of the evidence of identity that is required can be found in Practice Guide 67.

(2) Evidence of identity

Where any transferor, landlord, transferee, tenant, borrower or lender listed in (1) was not represented by a conveyancer

☐ I confirm that I am satisfied that sufficient steps have been taken to verify the identity of

----

----

and that they are the registered proprietor or have the right to be registered as the registered proprietor

☐ I enclose evidence of identity in respect of each unrepresented transferor, landlord, transferee, tenant, borrower or lender for whom I have not provided the confirmation above

| 14 | Where the application is sent to Land Registry by someone who is not a conveyancer |

(1) Details of conveyancer acting

If you are sending an application to register a transfer, lease or charge (ie a mortgage), for each party to each disposition that is to be registered, state in the table below the details of the conveyancer (if any) who represented them.

You must also complete (2) below.

If the party is not represented insert 'none' in the second column.

Name of transferor, landlord, transferee, tenant, borrower or lender	Conveyancer's name, address and reference
	Reference:
	Reference:
	Reference:

If you are sending an application to give effect to a discharge in Form DS1 or release in Form DS3, for each lender state in the table below the details of the conveyancer (if any) who represented them.

You must also complete (2) below.

Name of lender	Conveyancer's name, address and reference
	Reference:
	Reference:

(2) Evidence of identity

☐ for each applicant named in panel 6 is enclosed

☐ for each unrepresented transferor, landlord, transferee, tenant, borrower or lender listed in (1) is enclosed

15

Signature of conveyancer: _____

Date:

OR

Signature of applicant: _____

Date:

WARNING
If you dishonestly enter information or make a statement that you know is, or might be, untrue or misleading, and intend by doing so to make a gain for yourself or another person, or to cause loss or the risk of loss to another person, you may commit the offence of fraud under section 1 of the Fraud Act 2006, the maximum penalty for which is 10 years' imprisonment or an unlimited fine, or both.

Failure to complete this form with proper care may result in a loss of protection under the Land Registration Act 2002 if, as a result, a mistake is made in the register.

Under section 66 of the Land Registration Act 2002 most documents (including this form) kept by the registrar relating to an application to the registrar or referred to in the register are open to public inspection and copying. If you believe a document contains prejudicial information, you may apply for that part of the document to be made exempt using Form EX1, under rule 136 of the Land Registration Rules 2003.

© Crown copyright (ref: LR/HO) 07/08

Land Registry
Disclosable overriding interests

DI

This form should be accompanied by either Form AP1 or Form FR1.

If you need more room than is provided for in a panel, and your software allows, you can expand any panel in the form. Alternatively use continuation sheet CS and attach it to this form.

Leave blank if this form accompanies an application for first registration.	**1** Title number(s) of the property:
Insert address including postcode (if any) or other description of the property, for example 'land adjoining 2 Acacia Avenue'.	**2** Property:
The information in panel 3 will help us if this form becomes detached. Insert the full name(s) of the applicant on Form AP1/FR1. Where a conveyancer lodges the application, this must be the name(s) of the client(s), not the conveyancer.	**3** This form is lodged with an application in Form AP1/FR1 made by:

The registrar may enter notice of a disclosed interest in the register of title.

You may use as many Forms DI as are necessary.

The plan to any certified copy lease must show all colours shown on the original.

Notice of lease(s) will only be cancelled on receipt of a Form CN1 with evidence of determination.

If two or more leases of the same property and the same date are listed, include a number or other identifier for each lease in the first column.

4 List below all unregistered disclosable leases in date order, starting with the oldest.

Lodge a certified copy of either the original or counterpart of each lease disclosed.

	Description of land leased	Date of lease	Term and commencement date
e.g.	Flat 1, garage 3 and bin store	24.06.2008	5 years from 24.06.2008

	5	List below any disclosable overriding interests other than leases. Lodge any documentary evidence within the control of the applicant that identifies the interest disclosed.

For each interest disclosed in this panel:

Give a description of the interest, for example, a legal easement.

Give details of the deed or circumstance in which the interest arose.

Complete only if the interest affects part of the title. Give a brief description of the part affected, for example 'coloured brown on the attached plan'.

a.

arising by virtue of:

affects the part(s) of the registered estate as shown:

b.

arising by virtue of:

affects the part(s) of the registered estate as shown:

c.

arising by virtue of:

affects the part(s) of the registered estate as shown:

Completion information and requisitions on title

WARNING: Replies to Requisitions 4.2 and 6.2 are treated as a solicitor's undertaking.

Address of the property

Postcode ☐☐☐☐☐☐☐☐

Seller

Buyer

This form should be completed and read in conjunction with the explanatory notes available separately

1 Property information

Is the seller aware of any change in the written information given by and on behalf of the seller prior to exchange of contracts or have you become aware of any changes? (This includes any information in the TransAction forms, the Home Information Pack, replies to other pre-contract enquiries, correspondence between us and, if appropriate, replies to any requisitions on title already raised).

☐ Yes ☐ No ☐ Enclosed
☐ Given below

If Yes, please give details:

The Law Society

www.hips.lawsociety.org.uk

TA13

© Law Society 2007
Peapod Solutions Ltd

2 Vacant possession

2.1 If vacant possession (of whole or part) is to be given on completion:

  (a) What arrangements will be made to hand over the keys?

will be left with agents

will be left with seller's solicitors

other (please give details)

  (b) By what time will the seller have vacated the property on the completion date?

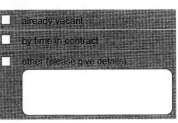

already vacant

by time in contract

other (please give details)

2.2 If vacant possession (of whole or part) is not being given, please confirm that an authority to the tenant to pay the rent to the buyer will be handed over or be included with the documents to be remitted to the buyer's solicitors on completion.

Confirmed

3 Deeds and documents

3.1 If the title is unregistered, do you hold all of the title deeds?

Yes   No

If No, please give details:

3.2 Please supply a list of the deeds and documents to be handed over or remitted to the buyer's solicitors on completion.

Enclosed

4 Completion

4.1 Will completion take place at your office? ☐ Yes ☐ No

If No, where or how will it take place?

WARNING: A reply to requisition 4.2 is treated as an undertaking. Great care must be taken when answering this requisition.

4.2 If we wish to complete through the post, please confirm that:

    (a) You undertake to adopt the Law Society's Code for Completion by Post; and ☐ Confirmed

    (b) The mortgages and charges listed in reply to 6.1 are those specified for the purpose of paragraph 3 of the Code. ☐ Confirmed

5 Money

5.1 Please state the exact amount payable on completion.

£

If it is not just the balance purchase money, please provide copy receipts for any rent or service charge or other payments being apportioned.

☐ Enclosed ☐ Not applicable

5.2 Please provide details of your bank and the account to which completion monies are to be sent:

Name of bank

Address of bank

Branch sort code

☐☐ ☐☐ ☐☐

Client account name

Client account number

Completion information and requisitions on title **TA13**

6 Mortgages and charges

6.1 Please list the mortgages or charges secured on the
property which you undertake to redeem or discharge
to the extent that they relate to the property on or before
completion (this includes repayment of any discount
under the Housing Acts).

**WARNING: A reply to requisition 6.2 is treated as an undertaking. Great care must be taken
when answering this requisition.**

6.2 Do you undertake to redeem or discharge the
mortgages and charges listed in reply to 6.1 on
completion and to send to us Form DS1, DS3,
the receipted charge(s) or confirmation that notice
of release or discharge in electronic form has
been given to the Land Registry as soon as you
receive them?

☐ Yes   ☐ No

6.3 If you agree to adopt the current Law Society's Code
for Completion by Post, please confirm that you are
the duly authorised agent of the proprietor of every
mortgage or charge on the property which you have
undertaken, in reply to 6.2, to redeem or discharge.

☐ Confirmed

7 Additional requisitions

Additional requisitions not raised prior to exchange
are attached:

☐ Yes   ☐ No

**WARNING: These replies should be signed only by a person with authority to give
undertakings on behalf of the firm.**

Buyer's solicitor

Date ☐D☐D / ☐M☐M / ☐Y☐Y

Seller's solicitor

Date ☐D☐D / ☐M☐M / ☐Y☐Y

TA13 *Completion information and requisitions on title*

www.hips.lawsociety.org.uk

Additional requisitions not raised prior to exchange

Completion information and requisitions on title TA13